D0629231

ARNULFO L. OLIVEIRA MEMORIAL LIBRARY
1825 MAY STREET
BROWNSVILLE, TEXAS 78520

THE STRANGE DESTINY
OF RUPERT BROOKE

The STRANGE DESTINY of RUPERT BROOKE

John Lehmann

HOLT, RINEHART AND WINSTON
NEW YORK

ARNULFO L. OLIVEIRA MEMORIAL LIB
1825 MAY STREET
BROWNSVILLE, TEXAS 78520

Copyright © 1980 by John Lehmann

All rights reserved, including the right to reproduce
this book or portions thereof in any form.
First published in the United States in January 1981
by Holt, Rinehart and Winston, 383 Madison Avenue,
New York, New York 10017.
Originally published in Great Britain under the title
Rupert Brooke: His Life and His Legend.

Library of Congress Cataloging in Publication Data
Lehmann, John, 1907–
The strange destiny of Rupert Brooke.
First published under title: Rupert Brooke, his life
and his legend.
Includes index.
1. Brooke, Rupert, 1887–1915—Biography. 2. Poets,
English—20th century—Biography. I. Title.
PR6003.R4Z69 1980   821'.912 [B]   80–17419
ISBN 0–03–057479 X

First American Edition

Printed in the United States of America
1 3 5 7 9 10 8 6 4 2

Contents

516.04 B67 $12.81 7d Second Se

Illustrations

(following page 82)

Rupert Brooke with his brother Alfred
Rupert's mother, 'the Ranee'
Rupert as schoolboy cricketer
The Herald in the *Eumenides*
The Attendant Spirit in *Comus*
Noel Olivier
Brynhild Olivier with Justin Brooke
Rupert Brooke in the New Forest
The Old Vicarage, Grantchester
Rupert on the Cam with Dudley Ward
The announcement of the new House Master at School House,
    January 1910
Rupert at work, outside the Old Vicarage
Edward Marsh, a drawing by Violet, Duchess of Rutland
Jacques Raverat, painted by Gwen Darwin
Ka Cox in 1912
Ka Cox, a drawing by Henry Lamb
A poem written by Rupert in Edward Marsh's Commonplace
    Book
Rupert in Ottawa with Duncan Campbell Scott
Taata Mata
Cathleen Nesbitt
Rupert with members of the Hood Battalion of the Royal Naval
    Division
Rupert's first grave on Skyros
The memorial plaque in Rugby School Chapel

Preface

Nobody can write about Rupert Brooke today without acknowledging an immense debt to the late Christopher Hassall, whose monumental biography, nearly a quarter of a million words in length, was published in 1964; unfortunately his sudden death a year earlier did not allow him to revise it.

The almost equally great debt a new biographer must acknowledge is to Sir Geoffrey Keynes, Rupert Brooke's lifelong friend since his schoolboy days and last survivor of his original literary executors, who is responsible for the edition of the collected *Poetical Works*, first published in 1946 and revised in 1974; and the selected *Letters*, published in 1968.

With Hassall's biography and Sir Geoffrey's edition of the letters, almost every day-to-day detail of Brooke's short life can be followed, his activities, his developing interests, his friendships, his love affairs, and his writings. Nevertheless a number of books, particularly of reminiscences, have since appeared, which enlarge the portrait in several important aspects, and in some cases alter the perspective in which Hassall saw his hero; while many letters, which Sir Geoffrey chose not to use or was unable to consult, and are now available to the student, tend in the same direction. At the same time it must be emphasized that even now there are many crucially significant letters (such as those written to the Olivier sisters) which, for reasons which one must respect, are still withheld from view, and without which no picture of the author can be complete.

This book is neither a further essay in hagiography, nor an attempt to demolish its subject in his many and varied non-poetical literary manifestations which those who have ceased to worship at his shrine as the supreme soldier-poet of the

1914–18 war are perhaps inclined to undervalue, at least in their promise. Deeply influenced as I have been in my life by the war poetry which was written after his death, and which is associated with the names of Wilfred Owen, Siegfried Sassoon, Isaac Rosenberg and their contemporaries, it is impossible for me, as I believe for my generation as a whole, to treat as almost sacred the 1914 Sonnets which epitomized that popular mood that preceded Sassoon's *Counter-Attack*. Rupert Brooke was nevertheless a gifted though flawed poet of uneven quality, who might have grown considerably in stature if he had not died in the Aegean in 1915. He was one of the leaders of the Georgian movement which, though it is more mocked now for its frailties than appreciated for its achievements, and has been cast into the shade by the profound change of taste that must be linked primarily with the name of T. S. Eliot, was in many ways revolutionary in its day. He had such vigour of mind and wide-ranging intellectual interests that it is difficult not to believe that he would have continued to make his mark in some sphere or other of literature, even if poetry had ceased to be his main preoccupation. As a critic of books, plays and pictures, he was already remarkable in his later Cambridge days; as a travel-writer, observant, polished and witty with an engaging gift for picturesque description of places and people; and as a writer of letters, when his mind was not distorted by bitter passion or prejudice, delightfully frank and immediate, so that one feels that one can hear his living voice, fondly teasing, cajoling, pouring out affection, love and scorn without self-conscious premeditation, and in his arguments more often playful and fanciful than snubbing or contemptuous.

All this I have tried to judge with fairness, while giving precise reasons for an assessment of his poetry very different from that which held sway for so long. Never having seen him or known him, in fact having been far too young during his lifetime to have moved in any circle where he might have been encountered, it has been all the easier for me to discount the magnetic effect his charm and sensational good looks had on so many of his contemporaries, which blinded them so often, not merely to the imperfections of his poetry, but also to the darker side of his character. For that this darker side undoubtedly existed has emerged more clearly from much that has been published in recent years of his own letters and from reminiscences of those who knew him personally, and has had to be admitted now even by those who have been his most devoted admirers. To take one plain instance of the two attitudes, his loving friend and patron, Sir Edward Marsh, wrote in his last volume of memoirs, *A Number of People*: 'My friendship with Rupert Brooke was certainly one of the most memorable things in my life. In his combination of gifts, of body, character, mind and spirit, he was nearer completeness and perfection than anyone I have known; intellect and goodness, humour and sympathy; beauty of person and kindness of heart, distinction of taste and the "common touch", ambition and modesty, he had them all; and there is no telling what he might have done if he had lived.' Virginia Woolf, on the other hand, who was fascinated by him in their youthful meetings and who, in her long notice of his *Collected Poems* in the *Times Literary Supplement*, also suggested that it was impossible to tell what direction his astonishing energies might have taken, was far from sharing this ideal view. A close friend of both Ka Cox and James Strachey, once very close to his heart but with whom his relations became so confused and often embittered after the emotional crisis at Lulworth, she made an entry in her diary for 28 July 1918 that she had gone to meet James on the 24th to hear his views on Rupert before she wrote her article. The conversation was, however, taken up by his news of Ka Cox's engagement to Will Arnold-Forster, and as James had to leave for a medical examination there was very little chance for him to discuss the intended subject with her. 'We couldn't say much about Rupert, save that he was jealous, moody, ill-balanced, all of which I knew, but can hardly say in writing.'

There is a clash of views here of an extreme sort. I have in this book endeavoured to explore Rupert's psychological history, and to record and to document, if not completely to elucidate this strange dichotomy in the judgement of him by close friends who knew him well, both before and after the disastrous breakdown he suffered in 1912.

I am particularly grateful to Sir Geoffrey Keynes for allowing me to study, and to quote from, the letters Rupert Brooke wrote to Ka Cox which are still preserved in their entirety, a large number unpublished, and are held in the magnificent

Rupert Brooke archive in King's College Library, Cambridge.
And I must thank the Librarian, Mr Peter Croft, and his Assistant Librarian, Mr Michael Halls, for their unfailing courtesy and
help in my researches. I must also thank the Curator of the
Henry W. and Albert A. Berg Collection in the New York
Public Library, Mrs Lola Szladits, for making available to me
the correspondence between Rupert Brooke and James Strachey
(both sides) which is now no longer reserved, and for her so
perceptive sympathy throughout.

In addition, I must express my appreciation to the Arts Council of Great Britain for most valuable help, particularly in the
travels made necessary in the preparation of this book.

It is my personal regret, which I cannot help mentioning
in conclusion, that so many of Rupert Brooke's friends and
acquaintances, who were also my own at a later date, were
no longer alive when I began my work. How much easier, how
much more stimulating it would have been for me if I had been
able to discuss Rupert with – to name only a few – James and
Lytton Strachey, Virginia Woolf, Andrew Gow and Lady Violet
Bonham-Carter.

For the quotations which I have used in my text, my warmest
thanks to the authors, or their heirs and executors, and the
publishers of the following books:
The Letters of Rupert Brooke, edited by Sir Geoffrey Keynes
(Faber and Faber); *Heroes' Twilight* by Bernard Bergonzi
(Constable); *Winston Churchill as I Knew Him* by Lady Violet
Bonham-Carter (Eyre & Spottiswoode and Collins); *The Golden
Echo* and *The Flowers of the Forest* by David Garnett (Chatto
and Windus); *Lytton Strachey* by Michael Holroyd (Heinemann);
English Poetry of the First World War by John H. Johnston
(Oxford); *Men Who March Away* with an introduction by Ian
Parsons (Chatto and Windus); *The Weald of Youth* by Siegfried
Sassoon (Faber and Faber); *First World War Poetry*, edited by
Jon Silkin (Penguin Books); *Beginning Again* by Leonard Woolf
(The Hogarth Press); *Books and Portraits* by Virginia Woolf
(The Hogarth Press).

For quotation from other material acknowledgments are due
to the following: The Provost and Scholars of King's College,
Cambridge (E. M. Forster letters); Patric Dickinson; Laurence
Pollinger and the Estate of the late Mrs Frieda Lawrence

Ravagli (D. H. Lawrence letters); the Society of Authors as agents for the Strachey Trust (Lytton Strachey letters).

I would also like to express my warm appreciation of the help Miss Cathleen Nesbitt has given me. And of the care in the preparation of the book given me by Mrs Lesley Hawtree and Mr Christopher Hawtree.

Part One

I

The Crisis at Lulworth

In the last days of December 1911 the young poet Rupert Brooke, then in his twenty-fifth year, travelled down to Lulworth on the Dorsetshire coast to join a group of Cambridge friends who had arranged a reading party there, and were staying in scattered lodgings. He had just published a first book of poems, and had put the finishing touches to a thesis on the Elizabethan dramatist John Webster, with which he hoped to be elected a Fellow of his old College, King's. He had, in fact, been working too hard, and was both nervously and physically exhausted. His health had never been particularly robust, and he was subject to recurrent feverish collapses and also to eye trouble.

Rupert Brooke had had a notable undergraduate career at Cambridge, both socially and intellectually, even if the many pursuits he had eagerly involved himself in had caused him to neglect his academic studies during his first three years. Everyone knew him, or wanted to know him and be associated with him. He was especially prominent in the amateur dramatic activities of a group which came to be known as the Marlowe Dramatic Society, though he had no particular gift as an actor himself. He had also been drawn into the activities of the University Fabian Society, and became its President in 1909. He was tall, nearly six foot, with exceptional good looks and a natural charm or magnetism to which almost everyone he met, male and female, succumbed. His beautifully sculptured head, set on a long neck, his abundant reddish-gold hair and deep-set blue eyes, and his peculiarly delicate rose-tinted complexion could not fail to attract, though some more exacting connoisseurs of male beauty have maintained that the eyes were just a trifle too small, and the legs not quite long enough, or even quite straight enough to complete the ideal effect of his physical appearance. Many, nevertheless, are the tributes to the startling impression he made. The novelist David Garnett, a contemporary, has written of his 'careless animal grace and a face made for teasing and sudden laughter.' And one sober observer, never given to exaggerated enthusiasm, Leonard Woolf, has said: 'His looks were stunning – it is the only appropriate adjective. When I first saw him, I thought to myself: "That is exactly what Adonis must have looked like in the eyes of Aphrodite".' Leonard also added that he thought Rupert had a ruthless, even cruel streak in him. E. M. Forster, in a letter to Malcolm Darling, a few months after Rupert's death, also emphasized this other side to his character: 'He was essentially hard: his hatred of slosh went rather too deep and affected the eternal water-springs, and I don't envy anyone who applied to him for sympathy.'

The other friends who forgathered in or near Lulworth for the reading party just after Christmas included Rupert's old chum from his boyhood days at preparatory school, James Strachey, and James's brother, Lytton, who was completing the work on his first published book, *Landmarks in French Literature*, for the Home University Library series; the handsome young painter Henry Lamb, for whom Lytton had recently conceived an intense (and frustrated) infatuation; Maynard Keynes, the future economist of world renown and a contemporary at King's; and Katherine Cox, known as Ka, who had been at Newnham while Rupert was at King's, and had become one of his intimate circle, joining him especially in his Fabian Socialist enthusiasms.

Ka Cox was an orphan; her mother had died when she was a child, and in her young girlhood she had had to help her elder sister look after family and home. Her mothering instincts were strongly developed, and though she was decidedly plain and rather heavily built, the aura she gave out of calm, protective sympathy exerted a powerful attraction on those who came to know her well. 'To be with her,' wrote one friend, 'was like sitting in a green field of clover.' Not long before she had suffered a severe reverse in love, and had since begun to be attracted to Henry Lamb, who, though already married, was never one to discourage the sexual interest of a nubile female. At the same time Rupert, though still emotionally involved with another, very young girl, had for some time been increasingly drawn to Ka, basking in her special solicitude for him to the very verge of love. A potentially explosive situation. A disastrous explosion did in fact occur. No one knows exactly what happened during that week-end. It has been alleged that Ka had specially asked Lytton to invite Henry Lamb, though it seems unlikely that Lytton needed any prodding to issue this invitation. In any case, Lamb had found rooms nearby with Augustus John and arrived at Lulworth some time on Saturday, 30 December, while Rupert had arrived on the Wednesday evening. In the late afternoon or evening of that Saturday it seems fairly certain that Ka disappeared with Lamb for a long walk by the sea-shore. There have been further speculations about the behaviour of these two during the week-end, but for want of corroboration they will have to be ignored. What we do know is that some time after the nocturnal walk, probably on the Sunday morning, Ka went to Rupert and told him she was in love with Lamb. To other explanations for this emotional surprise she added the fatuous one that Lamb had the same Christian name as her dead father – which makes one feel that she can have had no inkling of the havoc her revelation would cause in Rupert's breast.

A violent scene appears to have taken place between them, either on the Sunday or a day or two later. Rupert's latent hysteria, exacerbated by his state of exhaustion, flared up, and inflamed jealousy, in a not uncommon psychological pattern, immediately convinced him that he had been deeply in love with Ka, that she had betrayed him, and that to save him – and of course herself – she must consent on the spot to marry him. He was horribly wounded in his vanity, and perhaps in his sense of manhood, feeling that he had been taken advantage of by a callous philanderer. It seems likely that he at least suspected that Ka and Lamb had had sexual intercourse – and that at a time when he was suffering from prolonged chastity. Bewildered and profoundly alarmed by the storm she had conjured up, Ka objected; but half agreed to meet him in Munich, where he already had made plans to spend some time in the New Year, as in the previous January.

Henry Lamb left for London, as far as we can tell unaware of, or at any rate not particularly disturbed by, Rupert's demoralized state. On Monday, the first day of 1912, James

Strachey also left for London, and Rupert accompanied him on a long walk over the Purbeck hills to catch his train at Corfe Castle, pouring out his woes and trying to make his friend understand. It seems that James was dismayed and baffled by Rupert's ruthless accusations and allegations, particularly as they concerned his brother Lytton. Rupert himself left Lulworth soon after, fleeing for comfort into the arms of his newly married friends, Jacques and Gwen (Darwin) Raverat. They realized at once how serious his state of mind was, and took him to see a Harley Street specialist, Dr Craig, whose opinion it was that Rupert was 'obviously in a state of severe breakdown'. He recommended complete rest and a special diet in a place where he could find plenty of sunshine and a mild winter climate. As Mrs Brooke, his mother, was already staying in Cannes, the Raverats persuaded Rupert to leave almost at once, and arranged for a mutual friend to look after him between trains in Paris, and see that he caught the night express to the south. His mother was waiting for him at Nice station.

The strange obsession that Lytton Strachey, and not the obvious culprit, Henry Lamb, was responsible for the disaster, took a fixed, completely irrational hold on Rupert's mind. They had been friends for some time, had stayed with one another on more than one occasion, and though Lytton did not have quite the high opinion of Rupert's gifts that some of his other contemporaries had, there was certainly no shadow of jealousy or malice in his attitude. It was Lytton who had been his chief advocate for admission to the secret Cambridge Conversazione Society, known as the 'Apostles'. Rupert knew perfectly well that Lytton was homosexual and does not seem to have been in the least bothered by the fact, target though he was of the secret yearnings of many men of Lytton's persuasion.

It is not inconceivable that what really upset him was a hidden fear that Lytton and his friends thought that he was more attracted by his own rather than the other sex, and were not taking him seriously as a lover of women. There was certainly something almost girlish or at least ambiguous about his youthful looks. 'His clear, rosy skin helped to give him the look of a great girl,' wrote the poet Edward Thomas after his death. He acknowledged himself that he had a feminine side to his nature, which he put down to the fact that his mother had been longing to have a girl before he was born, and was much disappointed when she gave birth to a second son. At Rugby other boys fell in love with him, and he played up to them. It would have been hardly surprising if in the free sexual atmosphere of the circles in Cambridge into which he was drawn in his late teens he had been at least tempted to yield to homosexual experiments. There is, in fact, clear evidence from Rupert's own mouth (or rather hand) that at least one such episode took place when he was twenty-two. In July 1912 James had called his attention to the announcement in *The Times* of the death of a young man he called 'Denham', whom he knew to have been a very close friend of his. In his reply Rupert, astonishingly, gave an exact account of how he had seduced Denham one night when he came to stay with him at the Orchard in the autumn of 1909. He and Denham had, it appears, flirted and made amorous advances to one another, hugging and kissing as early as 1906; but nothing further had happened. On this autumn night at the Orchard, Rupert had come into Denham's room when they were both in their pyjamas, and lain on the bed beside him. He complained that he was cold, whereupon Denham invited him to come *into* the bed. Very soon Rupert was aware of strong sexual arousal, and told Denham to come with him to his own room. There they took off their pyjamas and made, what was impossible by now to restrain, violent love to one another. All that happened is described by Rupert in unashamed detail. When it was over, Denham returned to his room and Rupert was left anxiously surveying the mess they had made of the bed. When he accompanied Denham to the station next morning he was afraid that the boy would say that he never wanted to see him again; but he found that his mood of intimate affection was quite unaltered. There can be scarcely any doubt that this Denham was the young brother of his friend Hugh Russell-Smith, and had also been at Rugby with him. Whether they did, in fact, meet again before his death remains obscure.

Whatever the reason or suspicion about the events at Lulworth may have been, Rupert's obsession persisted. Cooler reflection might have made him see that Lytton, infatuated with Henry Lamb himself, could hardly have had a motive in deliberately engineering an affair between Ka and the young man he worshipped. But in his state of acute paranoia he was impervious to reason. Lytton's innocence on this count is surely proved by the letters, characteristically sensible and thoughtful

for others, which he wrote to Lamb at the time. On the 4th
January Lytton informed him that Ka had confided in him and
asked him whether he thought there was any chance of Henry
eventually marrying her. At first Lytton thought it might work;
but the more he considered it, the more doubtful he grew. 'I
can't believe you're a well-assorted couple – can you? . . . I
almost believe the best thing she could do now would be to
marry Rupert straight off. He is much nicer than I had thought
him.' Two days later he wrote: 'If you're not going to marry
her, I think you ought to reflect a good deal before letting her
become your mistress. I've now seen her fairly often and on
an intimate footing, and I can hardly believe she's suited to
the post. . . . I still think there's quite a chance that everything
might blow over, and that she might even sink into Rupert's
arms.'

At the same time he was well aware of Rupert's torments.
'The situation, though, seems to be getting slightly grim,' he
had written the day before. 'Rupert is besieging her – I gather
with tears of desperation – and sinking down in the intervals
pale and shattered.'

It seems unlikely that at this time Lytton realized that he
had been cast for the role of chief villain. At the beginning he
was sole villain. It was not till later that Rupert's paranoia,
drawing more and more people into its vortex, included the
whole of the group of intellectuals that was coming to be known
at this time as 'Bloomsbury', tainted at least by association.
Virginia Stephen (before she married Leonard Woolf a few
months later) was one of his close friends in the group. She
had played cricket with him as a child in Cornwall, and had
stayed with him and enjoyed midnight bathing with him, when
he was living in the Old Vicarage in Grantchester during the
summer of 1911. And when he got back to his home in Rugby
after his convalescence in Cannes, he wrote to her at the
beginning of March:

'Virginia dear, I'm told – in the third-hand muffled manner
I get my news from the Real World – that you've been, or
are, unwell. It's not true? Let me implore you not to have as
I've been having, a nervous breakdown. It's *too* unpleasant –
but you're one of the few people who, of old, know what
it's like. ("Hypersensitive and introspective," the good doctor

Craig said I was.) I feel drawn to you, in this robust hard world. What tormented and crucified figures we literary people are! God! How I hate the healthy unimaginative hard shelled dilettanti, like James and Ka. It was a pity you couldn't come to the House Party long, long ago at Lulworth – not that you'd have enjoyed it: it was *too* horrible. But you might have made all the difference. I fell into an abyss there. . . .'

His remark in this letter about his oldest friend, James Strachey, suggests that he was finding him imperfectly sympathetic in this crisis; but he continued to see him on an amicable basis, and write regular letters to him, though he may have been more than a little uncomfortable about the fact that he was the brother of his new *bête noire*. And when Maynard Keynes, a fellow Apostle, wrote from Cambridge in April to tell him that he wasn't going to get his longed-for Fellowship, but could anticipate a much better chance the following year, Rupert wrote him a friendly letter of thanks, and said: 'I didn't come to Cambridge: I wasn't fit. I'm not fit for anything. I have suffered a Seelenbruchenleide – or, as the sailor said to me last Thursday, I've done myself in.' He even added, as a postscript: 'Love to Duncan if you're at Brunswick [Square].' This was Duncan Grant, who had also been at preparatory school with him and James Strachey. He can hardly not have known that Keynes was at that time Duncan Grant's lover.

Once established at Cannes under his mother's care, supposedly wrapped in a cocoon of total rest, peace, and fattening up, Rupert began to bombard Ka by almost every post with frantic appeals to love him, to devote herself to him utterly, to rescue him from his anxieties and terrors, and to promise to be reunited with him at the very earliest possible moment, either in Munich (to which she had just gone) or some north Italian city, once he could square his mother or outwit her vigilance. Ka appears to have been rather frightened by this barrage of almost raving letters, and tried to humour him, without – at least in her secret self – giving up her feeling about Henry Lamb which now dominated her.

'You go burning through every vein and inch of me, till I'm

all Ka; and my brain's suddenly bursting with ideas and lines and flames, and my body's all for you,' he wrote in his first letter from Cannes. 'I'm more sane, a little, about the world. Oh, far from sane; but better. I'm convinced that sanity is the most important thing there is. I'm so hampered and spoilt because there are things I dare not face, and depths I daren't look into.' The more he thought about her in his isolation, the more she obsessed him. 'One gets worse and worse. You grow on one so. It's a pervading, irresistible thing, Ka. It's like having black beetles in the house. . . . So, I tell you, I get frightened. Where's it to stop? Am I to plunge deeper and deeper for ever?'

Some people, lost and tormented in such a spiritual crisis, might have turned to religious or mystical belief to support and calm them; but Rupert had none. While at Cambridge he had become a complete, in fact a militant, atheist. In a letter to Gwen (Darwin) Raverat, whom he suspected of weakening in her rationalist philosophy, he had written from Florence the year before:

'I implore you to extend the flickering fingers of derision at the sky. Did that vapid blue concavity make Brunelleschi build the Pazzi chapel? No! No! Derision's for God. But if it's really that madder horror, the Life-Force, that you're so anthropomorphically female to, even derision won't do. Laws do not wince. . . . But there aren't laws. There aren't. Take my word for it. I saw – I lifted up the plush curtain and looked behind – nobody, only dust and a slight draught from the left. (*Dust and a little draught* rhyme with *laughed* in the metrical version.) There are no laws; only heaps of happenings, and on each heap stands one of us and crows – a cock on a dung-heap on a beacon on a hill (in Lord Macaulay's poem) according to taste. . . .'

There was no letter from Ka for several posts, and he did indeed plunge even deeper. He began a long letter to her on Friday, 19 January: 'Damn! A Bad Night. It followed on Depression yesterday. For five hours yesterday I was convinced that it was all something right inside the head, and that I was either going to have a stroke, or else going slowly mad. It may be true: and one's so damnably helpless. . . . Yesterday (and part of today) I felt a cloud in my head and about me that seemed to mean it too certainly.' The next morning brought a letter from Ka at last, but it did him no good; it was, he wrote, as he finished the long outpouring, one of her 'tired, kind cold letters'. Why couldn't she give him the faith and strength he so desperately needed? If she were with him, even for an hour, all would be well. She alone understood his 'horrible nature' and had seen the 'dirty abyss' he had become. As he came to the end of the letter, he began to have qualms: that he had been too unfair, too selfish, that he ought not to post a letter that might make her even despise him, for being so wildly demanding and making himself out so helpless without her to comfort and reassure him. But he did post it.

And as soon as he had, he began to repent it. He started another long letter, trying to make it as calm and collected as possible, telling her about incidents in his day and people he was meeting. He rushed it off; and almost immediately, on the Monday morning, began yet another. He went out, leaving it unfinished. When he got back, he found a telegram from Ka. She had taken fright at his Friday letter and proposed to come to him in Cannes at once. He was horrified: horrified because he had worked on her sympathy so recklessly, and also – even more – because he didn't know how he would explain her arrival to his mother, who had no idea (or so he imagined) that he had been writing these frenzied love letters. He had to stop Ka. It was an absurd turn to events, but the vision of what would happen if she did come – even if he pretended to his mother that she was only stopping off *en route* to Italy – was too much for him. When he was with his strong-minded parent, he was still in part a little boy frightened of her finding out about his naughty goings-on. He dashed out, and sent a telegram to Ka in reply: 'Telegram partly unintelligible for heaven's sake don't come on account of me or my letters was mad and wicked other letters on way much better if however your own business can meet any train.' And he hurriedly finished the letter he had been writing to her: 'I diagnose that my beastly letter upset you. I'm worthy of treading to death in dung. I *was* ill, and am a bit; but I'm much better. I *will* get to Munich in a week. I'm really all right; only very rarely morbid. I'm so sorry.'

He waited, in nail-biting anxiety. Tuesday passed, and there was still no word from Ka. He began to imagine that his telegram and his letter had arrived too late: Ka would appear at the Hotel du Pavillon any moment, and all would be lost.

At last, on Wednesday evening, a cryptic telegram arrived, baffling, but at least it made it clear that she was still in Munich.

In a letter to James at about this time he confessed that for two days he thought he was really going mad; but also said he was sorry for the way he had behaved at Lulworth. Rather inconsequentially he added that he had noticed an exceptionally beautiful lift-boy in the hotel.

Once the danger of a confrontation between Ka and his mother had been avoided, the need to meet Ka and be with her became even more urgent. He found an excuse for going to Munich in the fact that the friend of his boyhood, Hugh Russell-Smith, was there. He insisted. He went to Thomas Cook about tickets. His mother, although deeply suspicious by now and deeply anxious about her son cutting short his convalescence so soon, gave way with a good grace in the end; feeling, wisely, that to put her foot down would only make Rupert's condition worse. She provided him with money for the journey. He arranged to meet Ka half-way, in Verona. On Tuesday, 30 January, just before noon, they were reunited on the platform of Verona station.

It is possible that, in his excited state of self-deceiving hysteria, Rupert thought that all would be well once he and Ka were, physically, together again. If so, he had misjudged Ka, and the strength of her infatuation for Henry Lamb. Nevertheless it seems certain that it was during this reunion that Ka yielded to Rupert's importunities and went to bed with him : Rupert's letters afterwards began to be full of intimate sexual references. That she had a child, still-born, which must surely have been his, is also known and confirmed by Cathleen Nesbitt.

The meeting started, therefore, well. They explored the monuments of Verona together, and then went back to Munich and the Carnival Ball. From there they made an expedition to Salzburg, and Rupert began, though with ups and downs, to recover his strength and self-confidence again. 'I really rather believe she's pulled me through,' he wrote to James Strachey. 'As the flood subsides I totter round.' But Ka had still a confession to make to him.

They decided to spend a week-end on the Starnberger See. They had been reunited for seventeen days, and Ka, seeing his reviving health and spirits, felt that she must, and could, at last tell him the truth. Apparently it was on the platform of

Munich station, while waiting to catch the train, that she found her opportunity and let him know that while he had been in Cannes, and before she left for Munich herself, she had been meeting Henry Lamb. Yes, she was in love with him. They had been together at a house-party, quite possibly at Lady Ottoline Morrell's house at Garsington, near Oxford; and Lytton Strachey and other members of the Bloomsbury set had been among the guests.

Rupert was shattered, and plunged straight back into the abyss from which Ka thought she had rescued him. It was not out of malice that she had told him about the house-party, but, following the code of frankness that had always existed between them, she was certain that she had to sooner or later. The trip to Starnberg was a disaster. An acquaintance of Rupert, whom they called on, recalled him as taking pills and medicated drops at frequent intervals, and looking ghastly. He then caught a chill, and became feverish. Out of her deep maternal nature, Ka gave him all the comfort she could. She partly succeeded, so that they were able to return to England four days later. Rupert, still incapable of accepting the stark truth, persuaded Ka to join him in Berlin a month or two afterwards. They would try again. Perhaps they could marry after all. Meanwhile he would live at home in Rugby, mainly under his mother's care, as quietly as he could.

The story of the next few months is confused. Rupert went to visit friends, stayed with James Strachey at the Mermaid Club in Rye, from where he wrote letters to Ka which are remarkable for the return of the old note of trusting love, whether whole-hearted or not. He finally went to see her at her home, where they worked out a plan for her to stay a week-end in Rugby and be introduced at last to his mother. The scheme was extremely tricky: all Rupert's childish fears of his mother revived; he tried several times to broach the subject, but each time his courage failed him. In the end he succeeded, and she agreed.

The visit was not a success. Another row obviously broke out between Ka and Rupert, as it had on the trip to Starnberg, and Ka left in a hurry, giving Rupert's mother what excuse we do not know. It was unfortunate that after this neither of them had the sense to abandon the plan to be reunited once more in Germany. For a strange thing was happening. Rupert's feelings, perhaps from a greater emotional exhaustion than he realized, suddenly began to cool. At the same time Ka began to lose her obsession about Lamb, and her feelings became more deeply involved with Rupert; not maternal solicitude any longer, but – at last and too late – love.

The revolution in their relations is only too clear in Rupert's letters from Germany. He left England at the end of April, and was joined a little later by Ka. Soon after, in a letter to his friend Dudley Ward, he wrote that she

'has climbed down a lot about Lamb. Tonight she said she didn't feel much interest in him now ... She'd promise never to see him again, she says, if we married. And I'm pretty sure she'll marry me, if I want. The crux is that that absolutely dead feeling I had when I was in Berlin before she came, hasn't vanished. I was afraid, beforehand, I might – when I saw her – be dragged down into the helpless tortured sort of love for her I had all the first part of the year, and had just crept out of. The opposite. I remain dead. I care practically nothing for any person in the world. I've anxiety, and a sort of affection for Ka – but I don't really care.'

Towards the end of May, he wrote an even more explicit – and, one cannot help feeling, selfishly callous – letter to Jacques Raverat. Ka and he were on a week's walking tour in the environs of Berlin.

'We lived in the present; only twice, shortly, mentioned past things,' he told Raverat. 'But you know, I was and am still dead (especially towards her). I go *about* with the woman, dutifully. I've a sort of dim, reflected, affection for something in her. But it's all sufficiently dreary. I can get up a sort of pity when I see how weak she is. But that won't do. Love her? bless you, no: but I don't love anybody. The bother is, I don't really *like* her, at all. There is a feeling of staleness, ugliness, trustlessness about her.... I thought things'd wake, if I went on. But I only seem to get deader. I've a sort of hunger for cleanness.'

At the end of the letter, he added something that shows only too clearly the way his thoughts were turning against Bloomsbury: 'I gather Noel went to Virginia's for a week-end. I suppose she's got too much sense – and she's got you and other wise people – to get spoilt in any way by the subtle degradation of the collective atmospheres of the people in those regions – people I find pleasant and remarkable as individuals.'

It was this Noel – Noel Olivier, the very young girl who had fascinated him so deeply before the imbroglio with Ka started – who began to occupy his guilt now. She was the youngest of the four daughters of Sir Sydney Olivier, then Governor of Jamaica, and Rupert had first met her, a schoolgirl from Bedales, at a party in Cambridge. David Garnett was a childhood friend of the Olivier girls, and he describes in *The Golden Echo* how they appeared to his youthful eye:

'I put Noel first and apart, because for me, and many others, she became more important than any of the family. But I did not realize that for a few years. She was quiet and the least conspicuous of the four sisters. Margery, the eldest, was tall, brown-eyed and brown-haired, handsome with the impulsive warmth and sudden chilliness of her father, an Olivier in temperament and character. Brynhild was the out-standing beauty of the four and grew into the most beautiful young woman I have ever known. She was rather fairer than Margery; with the most lovely bone structure, a perfect com-plexion with red cheeks, and starry eyes that flashed and sparkled as no other woman's have ever done. Daphne was darker, more dreamy, and, in her childhood, wrapped in the skin of some beast, or crowned with flowers, was exactly as I have always imagined several of Shakespeare's heroines – she was Ophelia, Perdita, Juliet and the Gaoler's daughter in *The Two Noble Kinsmen*.'

After the first meeting in Cambridge a correspondence began between Rupert and Noel, and he contrived that they should meet as frequently as possible, in spite of the jealous guardian-ship of her older sister Margery, who warned Rupert of the impossibility of what he was attempting. Nevertheless, in the summer of 1910, at a camp near Buckler's Hard in Hampshire, he managed to make a declaration of love to her, and found to his joy that his feelings were reciprocated. He wanted to announce at once that they were engaged, but Noel persuaded him to keep it secret.

He had, he realized, deeply engaged her affections, and then had grossly neglected her when he started to think of Ka as a future wife. His callousness was beginning to torture him, especially as there is no evidence that Noel herself did anything but try to be gently understanding, without reproaches about the course of events during the first six months of the year. 'Among a hundred horrors,' he wrote to Frances Cornford, who had been his confidante for so much of the time, 'I had been so wicked towards Noel, and that filled me with self-hatred and excess of feeling seeking some outlet.'

At the end of June he came back to England, and installed himself at the Old Vicarage in Grantchester, about which he had written his well-known poem even while he was most completely ensnared in his tangle of emotions in Berlin. It is probably his most popular poem: it is also one in which he shows, for the first time to the full, his exceptional gift for light verse. Written in the octosyllabics which from now on were to become his favourite form (except for the sonnet), it is light-hearted and witty; nostalgic, comically satirical and fantastical by turns – and extremely skilful throughout.

A few weeks later he joined a house-party near Oxford, which included James Strachey, Geoffrey and Maynard Keynes – and Noel Olivier. It appears to have been a high-spirited occasion; but Rupert was taking strong sedatives. He had made up his mind that he must meet Ka, and have it out with her. One of his closest Cambridge friends, Justin Brooke, who had a car, arranged the meeting, out in the countryside away from everyone. Rupert and Ka disappeared over the fields, and Justin Brooke waited for three or four hours. At last they reappeared, leaning against one another, evidently shattered by what they had gone through. That night Rupert wrote to the Cornfords; 'I can't love her, you see. So now it's all at an end. And she's passed out of my power to help or comfort. I'm so sad for her, and a little terrified, and so damnably powerless.' Their correspondence did not cease. Sometimes his old feelings of devotion and dependence seemed to revive, sometimes his bitterness suddenly dominated his mood again, when he sent her terrible letters. So terrible that they make one feel that he was indeed on the verge of madness – or of suicide, which he mentioned frequently. In the early autumn of 1912 he wrote her a letter going over the whole affair again, including his fruitless attempt after the crisis to attach himself to Noel once more;

and maintaining that he saw her as a *criminal* for what she had done to him.

Towards the end of that month of August 1912, James Strachey came to stay with Rupert in Rugby. Rupert had evidently been brooding over the whole lamentable history, and the more he brooded, in what one can only call his paranoiac state, the more he became convinced that Ka's and his mutual Bloomsbury friends were the evil influence behind the disaster.

Obviously Ka's revelation on the way to Starnberg that she had met Henry Lamb again after he had left for Cannes, and in the company of Lytton and Lady Ottoline, came back to him and inflamed his disordered thoughts ever more wildly; though if he had been capable of dispassionate reflection he would have seen that, with Ka at the time completely infatuated with Lamb, no other villains were necessary. He reproached James again for Lytton's alleged role in his discomfiture; James hotly defended his brother, maintaining that such evil scheming was totally alien to him. The more they argued, the more extreme and unreasonable Rupert's attitude became, until all Bloomsbury friends, James himself, Duncan Grant and even Virginia to whom he had written so sympathetically a few months before, were lumped together among the accused and accursed. Finally James had to leave the house with Rupert's denunciations ringing in his ears. They continued to correspond, sometimes bitterly, each maintaining his point of view; they met at gatherings of the Apostles, or elsewhere, on various occasions; but the old trust and intimacy had gone out of their relationship. And yet his bonds with James remained strong: they see-sawed between love and contempt. In June 1912 James wrote to him, telling him how lonely he felt, and appealing for his love, as the one thing that could console and support him. Rupert wrote back, to assure him that he did love him and wanted to help him. And yet two months later they had quarrelled again about Lytton, and Rupert wrote him a furious and totally unbalanced letter, saying that he was a bugger and as a bugger he couldn't distinguish between good and bad or understand the actions and responsibilities of normal people: he had not grown up. James replied gently and teasingly to this attack, observing quietly that he regretted that Rupert's sorrows had turned him into a prig. In a letter to Ka in February 1913, Rupert wrote: 'I went to King's for the week-end. I

ARNULFO L. OLIVEIRA MEMORIAL LIBRARY

1825 MAY STREET

BROWNSVILLE, TEXAS 78520

hoped to meet Lytton and insult him. But there was only James, who is so defenceless that it is no sport kicking him, after a bit. Otherwise, the usual gang.' To Geoffrey Keynes, the following month, he could end a letter with the postscript: 'Spit on Bloomsbury for me.'

This Rupert seems almost unrecognizably far from the high-spirited and gentle-natured young charmer of the earlier Grant-chester days, described so fondly by his devoted friend of that time, Sybil Pye: 'To us who knew him in all his moods, this quiet elegance of behaviour gave special poignancy to the one which was likely soon to follow it – being, indeed, never long absent – I mean that wild and mocking gaiety so inseparable from pictures called up by his name. . . : His gay unembarrassed laugh of pleasure still rings in one's head – one knew so well the sound of it.'*

In Rupert's overheated imagination, Lady Ottoline Morrell, though strictly speaking she was only on the fringes of Blooms-bury, also became a part of the conspiracy. He had been intro-duced to her salon in the spring of 1910, and there is no doubt that Ottoline, always enthusiastic over a new literary or artistic talent, made him especially welcome; but unfortunately Henry Lamb was one of the young artists she cultivated. After the crisis, she was aware that Rupert was deeply suspicious of her; and, typically, meeting him at a party given for the Contem-porary Art Society, she went over to him to make peace. Rupert shook hands; but peace had *not* been made, as became all too clear a little later.

Rupert's travels to North America and the South Seas in 1913 and early 1914 did not bring any calmer consideration. An unfortunate incident took place in the summer after his return, to show that his hurts, real, or imagined as most of them were, still rankled. He had gone to Drury Lane to see the Russian Ballet. In the crowded foyer in the interval, he suddenly

---

* In his quotations from this piece in his book, Christopher Hassall takes some surprising liberties with the text. When it appeared in Desmond MacCarthy's *Life and Letters* in May 1929, A. S. F. Gow, one of Rupert's close contemporaries, scribbled a note to me: 'This is what I should call the ordinary dew-dabbling stuff. . . . R.B. would have thought it absurdly sentimental (or so I think).' Nevertheless, in spite of the dew-dabbling, it does give some remarkably vivid glimpses of Rupert at the time.

encountered Lytton, with a group of friends, including Ottoline, beside him. Lytton offered him his hand : Rupert refused it, and turned his back on all of them. There was no reconciliation after that, though I do not doubt that Lytton, the gentlest and most generous-minded of men, would have welcomed it if the chance had occurred. When, in 1915, the news came through of Rupert's death, Lytton was profoundly shaken, lamenting the fact that they had never come together again.

What took the place of Bloomsbury in Rupert Brooke's social world, was an entirely new set of friends; and it is difficult to escape the conclusion that they did his intellectual development precious little good. Christopher Hassall, his official biographer, takes the view that after the Lulworth crisis Rupert never recovered his objectivity and sense of proportion; and this is confirmed by Geoffrey Keynes. The rejection of his former Bloomsbury friends meant also the rejection of their attitudes to life : their agnosticism, their contempt for conventional moral standards, their revolutionary open-mindedness in all intellectual and social matters, their overriding interest in avant-garde innovations in the arts. The Stracheys and the Stephens, one might say, lost the fight against his late-Victorian upbringing and the ethics of the public school in which his father had been so distinguished a housemaster – and whose work he had himself taken on for a short while after his parent's death. Nor can one ignore the magnet-pull of his strong-minded puritan mother, whose disapproval he had so feared and so surreptitiously flouted in the early stages of the crisis (though he was already twenty-five). And the young Noel Olivier, who in a sense remained engaged to him after the fundamental break with Ka ? She had shared many of his and Ka's friends, against whom he had now turned so violently; she was in danger of being tainted by them, he thought in his feverish dismay; but he realized that she would never marry him now – little wonder, considering the cavalier way he had treated her – and that 'she rather dislikes me, and always will.'

2

The Early Years

We must now go back and delve into the past that formed this brilliantly gifted and bewitchingly comely, but emotionally unstable and doomed young man; doomed because he died miserably before he could emerge from the traumas of his youth and show the true extent of his intellectual powers, and doomed also because after his death he became the subject of a distorting legend, recklessly inflated by those who should have been his most loyal and understanding friends.

He was born at Rugby on 3 August 1887 and was christened Rupert Chawner Brooke, the second of three boys, though there had been a daughter, born between Rupert and his elder brother, who died in infancy. His father was a master at the school, and a few years after Rupert's birth was appointed in charge of a House called School Field. As in most public schools, both then and now, the Houses were independent units, in which the housemaster was a mixture of hotel-keeper, disciplinarian overseer and teacher. Rupert's father was lucky in having in this task a capable and energetic wife, who took on the whole management of the House, the provision of meals for the boys, the attention to their comforts and welfare, and the general house-keeping with the aid of a matron as second in command. Mrs Brooke was born Ruth Mary Cotterill, and was married to William Parker Brooke in Edinburgh while he was a master at the Scottish public school of Fettes. She was pretty, and had charm as well as intelligence, but underneath the prettiness and the charm was a firm and self-reliant character with a strong puritan streak.

When he was ten years old, Rupert became a day-boy at Hillbrow, only a hundred yards down the road from the public school. It seems to have been a rather spartan and dreary institution, with about forty pupils. Rupert disliked it, and was glad to get home every evening, in spite of which its cold, dusty corridors affected his always delicate health, giving him frequent attacks of pink-eye and inflammation of the throat. He did not particularly distinguish himself, but one important event occurred; he made friends with a boy of his own age, James Strachey, the brother of Lytton. Though James went to St Paul's and Rupert to his home school of Rugby after they had finished at Hillbrow, they remained intimates until the fatal events occurred in the New Year of 1912 which I have just related. Also at Hillbrow, though older than Rupert by more than two years, was James's cousin Duncan Grant, the future painter.

There is much to be said against the British middle-class system of education, by which the boys are removed from home and segregated from the other sex for long periods every year, from the age of eight or nine to eighteen or nineteen; but one thing to be said for it is that it loosens the influence of commanding or doting parents on a boy's psychology. This Rupert Brooke was not to experience, as he went straight from a day-boy's life at Hillbrow to School Field at the age of fourteen in 1901; and thus until he went up to King's he was always in the atmosphere of a home where his father had the authority of a schoolmaster and his mother was probably an even more domineering personality. He had a room to himself at the top of the house, but the isolation from his family which this was supposed to provide was more seeming than real, as he could always slip away into his parents' part of the house, and in particular be given immediate care in the continually recurring bouts of illness, high temperatures, sore throats and conjunctivitis.

As an all-rounder, good at his books and good at games, Rupert made a success of his career at Rugby, though one hesitates to say that he was exceptionally outstanding. Early on he played cricket in his House XI, and soon moderately distinguished himself also at rugger, playing first for his House and, before he left, for the School XV. What was remarkable, however, was his rapidly developing interest in poetry. He devoured the classics of English poetry, and began to write verse himself, first of all very much in the aesthetic style of the nineties, with Ernest Dowson as his ideal. With another boy, who had just won the School Poetry Prize, he started a supplement to the school magazine, devoted to literature and called *The Phoenix*. A powerful influence on these early stir-rings was, without doubt, exercised by a young man whose family were neighbours and clearly acquaintances of his parents. His name was St John Welles Lucas-Lucas: he was already twenty-five, had taken a degree in law at Oxford, and when he enters the scene had chambers in the Middle Temple. How he first came into contact with Rupert is a little obscure, but he wrote poems and novels and had no doubt heard of *The Phoenix* and the two boys who were running it. He rapidly became a good friend and mentor to the budding poet, and swayed his taste for many years.

He was a French scholar, soon to edit the *Oxford Book of French Verse*, and introduced Rupert not only to the 'decadent' English poets of the nineties, but also to Baudelaire and perhaps to Verlaine as well. He revered Oscar Wilde, whose trial and disgrace had taken place less than ten years before, as a leader of the revolt against the Philistines – and in effect against Vic-torianism in general. All this was heady wine to a young school-boy who already felt the need stirring in him to rebel against the establishment of his time. He wrote to his cousin Erica Cotterill in May 1904: 'I have fulfilled one of the ambitions of my life; I have met a real live poet, who has presented me with a copy of one of his books signed with his own hand. Of course, like all poets worth counting nowadays, he is Celtic and very melancholy.'

For a time the poetry Rupert was trying his hand at was deeply imbued with plangent Dowsonesque languor and post-Pre-Raphaelite affectations of sentiment, as in the poem he enclosed in a letter to Lucas from Rapallo, where he had been sent for his health, at the age of seventeen:

> Go, heart, and pluck beside the Path of Dreams,
> Where moans the wind along the shadowy streams,
> > Sad garlands wreathed of the red mournful Roses
> > And Lilies o'moonbeams.
>
> Strange blossoms faint upon that odorous air,
> Vision, and wistful Memory; and there
> > Love twofold with the purple bloom of Triumph
> > And the wan leaf of Despair....

It was a long time before he entirely freed himself from these affectations; but this phase in his enthusiasms at least brought him to a fervent admiration for Swinburne. *Atalanta in Calydon* became one of his most cherished poems, and he read a paper on it, to a sixth-form literary society called *Eranos*, which showed a remarkable appreciation of its technical subtleties.

The pose which he had adopted in his poetry spilled over into his private life. By his last year at Rugby the physical beauty, which was to be such a striking element in the impression he made on others during his mature youth, had already revealed itself. He had grown tall, and his face had lost its puppy-fat. He had begun to wear his abundant red-gold hair longer than at that time convention expected; and, one cannot help feeling, because he knew what effect it had. In public schools the hero-worship a young boy conceives for a boy at the top of the school, who is both good-looking and good at games, is too frequent a phenomenon to be considered other than normal. It came to his ears that a boy in another House had asked the school photographer for a copy of his portrait. He was at the time laid up with one of his bouts of pink-eye, and was not allowed to read. For something to occupy his time (so he told one of his friends) he began a secret correspondence, full of flowery Wildean phrases, with the boy he called sometimes Hyacinth, sometimes Antinous. He made a joke of it, characteristically, to the friend or friends he let into the secret, but the episode had undoubtedly stirred something in him; and to his younger adorer it may have meant, while it lasted, a more serious emotional awakening than he was prepared to admit in himself.

The boy who appears to have been his chief confidant in this affair was Geoffrey Keynes, born in the same year. He had already become a close friend, and was to remain so during his Cambridge career and indeed to the end of his life. His elder brother Maynard was already at Cambridge, where he was a friend of Lytton Strachey who was completing his fifth year at Trinity. Lytton's younger brother James, who had been at St Paul's while Rupert was at Rugby, now re-entered Rupert's life, and they began corresponding again. By this time it had been finally decided that Rupert's university should be Cambridge, and not Oxford as was originally planned. Hearing much about the bright, good-looking would-be poet from Rugby who was soon to join them, both from his own brother and from Maynard's brother Geoffrey, Lytton hatched a conspiracy. He had long been a member of the ancient and secret Conversazione Society, known as the Apostles, together with Maynard and their friend and contemporary Leonard Woolf. He kept a watchful eye on the freshmen, looking for recruits – if possible easy on the eye as well as outstanding in intelligence. The Stracheys had taken a house at Kettering for the summer. Rupert was lured there for a visit by James and, under various false pretences, was persuaded to give answers to a questionnaire testing both his general intelligence and his philosophical attitude towards the world. During the visit Lytton arrived and gave the unsuspecting candidate a personal inspection, making at the same time a careful study of the letters Rupert had written to James. His report to James was characteristically caustic on a number of points, but not by any means altogether unfavourable.

In the course of these exchanges Lytton began to refer to Rupert as 'Sarawak' or 'the Rajah'. It seems unlikely that there was even the slenderest tie of consanguinity between Rupert's family and the famous Rajah Brooke, but when Rupert heard of this fancy of Lytton's he immediately decided to call his mother 'the Ranee' among his friends, a nickname that persisted to the end.

In December 1905 Rupert, together with his friends Geoffrey Keynes and Hugh Russell-Smith, went up to Cambridge for their exams, and stayed in the Keynes household. Rugby did well : Rupert won a classical scholarship to King's, Russell-Smith to St John's, and Geoffrey an exhibition in natural science to Pembroke. And when Rupert became an undergraduate in the Michaelmas term of the following year he was soon invited to become an 'embryo' postulant for the Apostles; before his first year was out he had been 'born' as a full member of a Society in which, while it conferred secret honour, lurked, for an ambitious young man, the danger of a lasting conceit and sense of exclusive intellectual superiority.

3
Cambridge

In his first few weeks at King's Rupert felt depressed and lonely. He had been a notable and popular boy at the top of the school at Rugby; now he was nobody. It was also the first time in his life that, unlike the majority of his fellow students, his education had taken him away from home. This in itself made the adjustment to his new life especially difficult. He complained that he found it harder than he expected to make new friends; only Geoffrey Keynes and Hugh Russell-Smith, and even they were at different colleges, remained of his old close companions. He wrote to his friend Lucas:

> 'At certain moments I perceive a pleasant kind of peace in the grey ancient walls and green lawns among which I live; a quietude that does not recompense for the things I have loved and have left, but at times softens their outlines a little. If only I were a poet I should love such a life very greatly, remembering moments of passion in tranquillity; but being first and chiefly only a boy I am restless and unable to read or write.'

He was lucky in the dons to whom he was assigned for his studies and lectures. They were all young, all bachelors, and lived in College. Rupert found to his surprise that they treated the undergraduates as friends, and did not in the least think of themselves as superior beings in the fashion of schoolmasters. Outstanding among them were Walter Headlam, one of the great classical scholars of his time, the witty and engaging Nathaniel Wedd, a determined atheist and early Fabian, J. T. Sheppard, a man of fascinating personality and an electrifying lecturer, and Goldsworthy Lowes Dickinson, famous already for his philosophical disquisitions *The Greek View of Life* and

A Modern Symposium. It would be no exaggeration to say that they were all inspired, to a greater or lesser degree, by a dream of recreating the atmosphere and ideals of the Athens of Socrates in their University. They were basically agnostics if not atheists, pagans who had assimilated Christian ethics rather than Christian morals or metaphysics. With such ideals, there was a strong homosexual element in their attitudes. But it would be a mistake to see them as exclusively dedicated to the literary masterpieces of the Classical languages; Walter Headlam may well have first awakened Rupert Brooke's enthusiasm for the plays of John Webster and the lyrics of John Donne.

Rupert spent four years as a Cambridge student, though he had lodgings for a further year a few miles out at Grantchester, preparing the dissertation by which he was eventually to win his Fellowship at King's. These years were marked by a tremendous extension of his circle of friends and his intellectual horizon, above all by a steadily growing interest in drama and everything to do with the theatre, and in the socialistic ideas and activities of his time.

A chance meeting appears to have started his career in undergraduate dramatic activities. He had made the acquaintance of another young man with the name of Brooke, no relation, who was a third-year undergraduate at Emmanuel College. This Justin Brooke, a gifted and attractive-looking young man who remained his friend for many years, was the son of the founder of the Brooke Bond tea business. He had come up to Cambridge from Bedales, the well-known progressive school which laid great emphasis on music, literature and the acting of Shakespeare. It was co-educational, and encouraged country rambling and camping out: for their enthusiasm for such pursuits the pupils earned the nickname of 'dew-dabblers'. During that Michaelmas term of 1906 Justin Brooke was taking the part of the Pythian Prophetess (he always took leading female parts) in a production of Aeschylus' *Eumenides* which the Greek Play Committee had organized. He suggested to Rupert one day that he should come and watch a rehearsal at the A.D.C. Theatre. The leading role of Orestes was at that moment being rehearsed by A. D. Scholfield, a Kingsman in his fourth year. He noticed the shy unknown man in the stalls, and was struck by his appearance. It occurred to him that he might be brought into the play, and asked Justin to introduce him. The result was that Rupert agreed to take the part of the Herald. With no lines to speak, all he had to do was to look his comely self and appear to blow a blast on a property trumpet while a cornet player in the orchestra blew a simultaneous, real blast. He evidently made a striking figure, and several members of the audience commented on this youthful-looking freshman's appearance, including one who was to become an extremely important figure in Rupert's life, and whose first impression of Rupert in the play was never to leave him. Of Edward Marsh, more later.

It was also through Justin that he met Jacques Raverat, a Frenchman who had come up to Emmanuel from the Sorbonne as an advanced student, formerly a fellow-Bedalian with Justin, with whom he shared rooms outside College. Rupert and he at once found an affinity, and their friendship rapidly grew close and lasting. It was again through Justin that he became involved in a much more important theatrical enterprise than the Greek Play Committee's *Eumenides*: the founding of the Marlowe Dramatic Society. Justin and several of his friends had been fired by the appearance in Cambridge of the famous Irish Players from the Abbey Theatre to feel that something ought to be done to revitalize the English theatre, and in particular to re-introduce English poetic drama. Perhaps, it occurred to them, the staging of a play by the neglected Elizabethan dramatist, Christopher Marlowe, was the answer; all the more appropriate as *Dr Faustus* was the play set for the Pass degree that year. At one of the Irish plays Justin had met Charles Sayle, a bachelor in his early forties, who was under-librarian at the University Library, and was to become one of Rupert's inner circle of Cambridge friends. Sayle brought Justin into touch with the A.D.C. and pleaded with them to take up the new idea. The A.D.C., however, refused to be moved to co-operate, devoted as it was to farce. Justin saw that a new group would have to be formed, and would need official University sympathy. He talked it over with Rupert, who was immediately enthusiastic, and together they persuaded Andrew Gow, a slightly older ex-Rugbeian then at Trinity, to intercede for them with the authorities. The move was successful, and Gow roped in Francis Cornford, one of his tutors in Classics, who in turn persuaded his senior classical colleague at

Newnham, the distinguished Jane Harrison, to co-operate. It was too late in the term for rehearsals, and so it was decided that they should start after the long vacation, as early as possible in the Michaelmas term of 1907; meanwhile, however, roles were allotted. Justin took the leading part of Dr Faustus, and was to act as producer and stage manager as well, with Andrew Gow assisting in the management. Rupert's role was Mephistopheles, and among his special Rugbeian friends Geoffrey Keynes took the role of the Evil Angel, Hugh Russell-Smith Gluttony among the Seven Deadly Sins, and the outstandingly promising musician, Denis Browne (who was to remain a devoted friend of Rupert's to the end), the role of Lucifer. No women were allowed as yet by the University authorities to act with their male colleagues, though the active spirits of the new society were fully determined to bring them in as soon as official prejudices could be broken down.

The first performance took place at the A.D.C. Theatre on 11 November. A leaflet was distributed which announced that: 'should this performance prove successful, it is intended to form a Society in Cambridge for the production of other Elizabethan plays'. No actors' names were given. In the audience was E. J. Dent, who was to become an eminent musical expert, and was at that time a don at King's though he had only recently returned from a long absence abroad. He noted that Justin as Faustus looked absurdly young for his part, and that Mephistopheles spoke in a 'thick and indistinct voice' with his head concealed in a cowl. Rupert, never excelling as an actor and always much more active and effective behind the scenes in all practical matters, does not appear to have made any particular impression. But the production as a whole did: Dent found it suffused with the 'spirit of poetry', and the production made a small profit, enough to encourage the formal founding of the Marlowe Society. It was constituted in the New Year of 1908, with Rupert as President, Geoffrey Keynes as Secretary and F. M. Cornford as Treasurer.

Charles Sayle, who was by now more than a little infatuated with Rupert – he sent him birthday presents and invited him to tête-à-tête dinners – gave a supper party for the chief actors after the performance. A few days later Rupert called on him, found him out, but decided to wait. Sayle recorded the impression he had, when he eventually came home: 'Standing in my hall in the dark, and thinking of other things, I looked towards my dining-room, and there, seated in my chair, in a strong light, he sat, with his head turned towards me, radiant. It was another unforgettable moment. A dramatic touch. A Rembrandt picture. Life.'

The next production that the new Society planned, in which Rupert was to make a much more effective stage appearance, was *Comus*. The summer of 1908 was the tercentenary of Milton's birth, and the Master of Christ's, which had been Milton's college, prepared to mount a grand exhibition as part of the celebrations. He also wanted to have *Comus* acted in the college garden, near the mulberry tree that according to tradition Milton himself had planted. He called in Justin Brooke to help him hatch the plot. Justin immediately went in great excitement to tell Rupert, who was equally captivated by the idea, especially as he worshipped Milton's poetry. There was, however, one big risk in the project as the Master conceived it: what if it rained on the day? They decided to suggest to him that after the tercentenary banquet he should invite the guests to the New Theatre, where the production could easily – and without risk – be organized. The Master agreed to the plan, and work began with a will. Justin was going down, and could not be active; but Rupert, with characteristic zeal for the handling of practical problems, took on the job of stage-manager, as well as the role of the Attendant Spirit. The part of Comus himself was eventually given to Francis Cornford. The Society now decided to take a bold step, and invited women to collaborate not only in the preparations but also in the actual acting. In this way Rupert came to know intimately two of the Darwin clan in Cambridge, Frances, the poet, who was to marry Cornford, and her cousin Gwen who was to marry Jacques Raverat and make a distinguished name for herself as both wood-engraver and autobiographer. Both were to have considerable significance in Rupert's life thereafter.

It was quite a triumph for the new Society to have managed to produce *Comus* at all, but the critical reaction was mixed. More than one critic complained of a certain lack of theatrical animation in the production, as if reverence for Milton was almost fatally subduing the actors. Rupert was no natural stage actor, moved stiltedly, and though a reputedly excellent speaker of verse in small gatherings of friends, seemed often to be inhibited by self-consciousness in public. Nevertheless he made something of a success of the part, and was admired for his appearance and his clear delivery of the opening lines. Lytton Strachey wrote a sympathetic but not uncritical review in the *Spectator*, praising the absence of 'theatricality and false taste' and the evident 'high ideal of artistic achievement' and the sensitive feeling for the beauty of an essentially undramatic poem; but faulting the lack of contrast in tone. Of Rupert's peformance as the Attendant Spirit, he wrote:

'One of the few phrases in the whole masque which seems to have caught something of the fire and intensity of the great Elizabethans occurs in the splendid passage in which the Attendant Spirit describes how, as he was sitting in the wood, he heard the Lady's Song:

> I was all ear,
> And took in strains that might create a soul
> Under the ribs of death.

That is not only beautiful, but it is exciting; but as it was enunciated by the actor, one felt the beauty of it and nothing more. However to have accomplished this much is no small achievement.'

Rupert wore his 'short, spangled sky-blue tunic' to the dance that followed, a costume so tight that he didn't dare to sit down. Among the invited audience were Thomas Hardy, the Poet Laureate Alfred Austin, Robert Bridges, Laurence Binyon and the critic Edmund Gosse. As Gosse was leaving the theatre someone remarked to him: 'So at last you've heard *Comus*.' 'I have overheard it,' Gosse replied.

At the same time Rupert's interests and activities began to develop in other directions. One of the first fellow freshmen he made friends with was the son of a Canon of Windsor, Hugh Dalton (later to become an outstanding Labour politician), who had just arrived at King's from Eton. They discovered that they had poetic enthusiasms in common, in particular Swinburne's *Atalanta in Calydon*, and very soon they decided to found a small society together. They gave it the name of the *Carbonari*, after the revolutionary group in early nineteenth-century Italy with whose secret plottings Byron had at one time been associated. There was nothing emphatically political about the

Carbonari of King's, but Dalton was already interested in the socialist movement that had received a powerful fillip from the General Election results of 1906. By the beginning of 1907 Dalton had become a Fabian socialist, and one evening he took Rupert along to meet a Trinity man called Ben Keeling, who had finally persuaded him to take the plunge. Keeling was a lively and attractive personality, who was filled with enthusiasm for the young Fabian movement and with dreams of reforming English society in non-revolutionary ways. He came up to Trinity in 1905 to find that there was already a small Cambridge branch of the movement with half-a-dozen members; but after the Liberal victory in 1906 the membership began to grow. To become a full member one had to sign a declaration of beliefs and intentions called the Basis; but one could start by becoming an Associate as a fledgling stage. Dalton had signed the Basis, and urged Rupert to do the same; but Rupert, who had long been an admirer of William Morris's *Sigurd the Volsung* and had been led on from the poetry to read the Utopian fantasy of *News From Nowhere*, said to him: 'I'm not your kind of Socialist, I'm a William Morris sort of Socialist.' He was, however, beginning to read a number of other books which opened his eyes to the almost desperate problems of poverty and social inequality in Britain at the time, including an important book by his uncle Clement Cotterill, a retired schoolmaster, called *Human Justice for those at the Bottom from those at the Top*. He wrote this uncle a thoughtful letter, in which he declared:

'I am an Associate (not an actual Member) of the Cambridge Fabian Society, and have lately been coming across there a good many Socialists, both of the University and without, as well as unattached sympathizers like Lowes Dickinson. I wish I could get more of these, especially among the Fabians, to accept your definition of Socialism. Most of them, I fear, would define it as "Economic Equality", or "the Nationalization of Land and Food Production" or some such thing. In a private way I have some influence among some of them, and have been trying to urge on some of them a more human view of things; I shall be able to do so a good deal better and more clearly now. . . .'

Nevertheless, after several months of reflection and reading, he decided to sign the Basis, and in the Easter term of 1908 he became a full Member.

From that moment Fabian Socialism occupied a great deal of his thought and activities. Fateful for Rupert's future was the fact that the Cambridge Fabian Society had decided to admit members from Newnham and Girton: Katherine Cox, in her first year, had been made Treasurer, and among other female members was Margery, the eldest daughter of Sir Sydney Olivier. At the beginning of May, before the production of *Comus*, Ben Keeling gave a large supper party for the Fabians in Trinity. Among the invited guests was H. G. Wells; the guest of honour was Sir Sydney, who brought Lady Olivier with him and three of their daughters. The youngest, Noel, dark-haired and with something distinctly boyish at that time in her unusual looks, was only fifteen and a half. A broken coffee cup in Cornford's rooms after the supper party brought Rupert and Noel together, and they talked for the first time. It seems to have been a *coup de foudre*: Rupert was immediately captivated, and from that time onwards was obsessed by her. As I have already described, he made every effort to engineer meetings with her, mostly clandestine or by covert schemes made to look like chance meetings, until the occasion in 1910 at Buckler's Hard, when they agreed to their secret engagement. But it must have been also about this time that Ka Cox slipped almost invisibly into some inner room of his being, and began to warm it like a log fire so slow-burning that he was for a long time hardly aware of it.

In a state of total exhaustion after the excitements of *Comus*, Rupert was persuaded by his mother to go home to rest at Rugby, where he passed his twenty-first birthday; but he was already planning to join the Fabian Summer School at Llanbedr in Wales, the first of a number of annual visits. A party of his friends were to accompany him on this first visit: Hugh Dalton, James Strachey, Dudley Ward, a new friend from St John's who was to become one of his closest intimates, Arthur Waley, later to be famous as a translator of Chinese poetry, Gerald Shove, another Apostle, and of course Ben Keeling. They stopped off at Leominster, where the Webbs were staying for the summer, picked Rupert up there, visited Ludlow Castle to see the site of the original performance of *Comus* in 1634, and then all went on together to Wales. The School was a high-minded affair, with lectures on Tolstoy and Shaw as well as the Poor Law; nevertheless there appears to have been some high-spirited irreverent fooling at the expense of the fatally caricaturable Webbs.

About this time Rupert discovered the theme that was to engross him more than any other in his new-found Fabian ideals. A Royal Commission had been set up by the Balfour Government just before the 1906 General Election to enquire into the workings of the Poor Law, and recommend reforms. When the Report was ready, four members of the Commission dissented from it. They included Sidney and Beatrice Webb, who proceeded to prepare their own report, which they then published under the title of *The Minority Report of the Poor Law Commission*. It was a complex and carefully researched document, inspired by genuine human – and not dogmatic – concern for the plight of the lowest strata of society, and was in fact prophetic of many changes in the structure and spirit of the law which were to come about in ensuing decades. Beatrice Webb summed up the thinking behind it in her declaration that 'The universal maintenance of a definite minimum of civilized life becomes the joint responsibility of an indissoluble partnership in which the individual and the community have reciprocal duties.' Rupert, already awakened to these problems by his uncle's book, studied the *Minority Report* with intense absorption, and was deeply affected by the basic postulates of partnership and reciprocal duties, far more than any calculation of statistics, intellectual theories or legal niceties could have moved him.

The Webbs decided to found a society within the Fabians, to be known as the National Committee for the Prevention of Destitution, with the aim of publicizing the conclusions of the Minority Report and arousing the conscience of the nation to demand changes in the Poor Law in the direction it suggested. Rupert became an early member, as did Hugh Dalton and Ben Keeling, and with the prospect of becoming President of the Cambridge Fabians in October organized with them a series of meetings on the subject for the Michaelmas term. With the help of his committee, which consisted (after the departure of Keeling and Dalton) of Margery Olivier, Ka Cox, Francis Cornford and Gerald Shove, he made even more ambitious plans for the following year. One of the chief schemes was a tour of the south-west in a caravan with Dudley Ward during the Long Vacation. The caravan was lent by Hugh and Steuart Wilson of King's from whom they also borrowed the horse, Guy. Dudley Ward was instructed by Rupert to bring a whole library of books, poets and critics and Fabian tracts. The meetings were to be called on village greens as well as in the town, and for the meeting at Poole in Dorset a special poster was prepared, which proclaimed: 'Poole High Street, close to the Free Library. Principal speaker Mr. BROOKE. Questions invited. In support of proposals for Poor Law Reform. Sponsored by the N.C.P.D.' The chief aim of the two young speakers was to persuade their hearers that the aged, the sick, and the unemployed deserved a better deal than they were getting under the old Poor Law or would get under the proposals of the Majority Report. They maintained that there were two or three million persons living in destitution in the country, and the majority through no fault of their own. If they were rescued from their destitution, and given back their self-respect, they would be able to contribute to the production of wealth and the general prosperity of the country. Not only the people who governed England, but the English people as a whole must change the way they looked at the problem – must have a change of heart.

It is not known how many converts their ardent and carefully argued preaching produced. The tour ended at Winchester. After an interval – a momentous interval at Buckler's Hard – Rupert went on with James Strachey to the Fabian Summer School. His zealous activity does not seem to have impressed Beatrice Webb, who for some reason took against him, though she may not have shown it outwardly. 'The egotism of the young University man is colossal,' she noted. 'They don't want to learn, they don't think they have anything to learn.' In their impetuous debating ardour Rupert and his friends must have seemed to Mrs Webb to be showing impatience and conceit. But she was wrong to conclude that they 'don't want to learn'. They had learnt almost all they knew from the Minority Report.

In December 1910 Rupert gave a long address to the Cambridge Fabians on Democracy and the Arts. It was his last speech to them, a closely reasoned, intelligent and imaginative piece of work, in many ways prophetic of the thinking that was to bring about the creation of the Arts Council several decades later. His vision of the future, if the spirit of Democracy (in

Rupert's language it meant more what we mean by Social Democracy) prevailed, rested on these three contentions: '(1) Art is important, (2) The people who produce art at present are, if you look into it, nearly always dependent on unearned income, (3) We are going to diminish and extinguish the number of those dependent on unearned income.' Rupert assumed without hesitation that when the 'national will' declared itself it would demand the expropriation of the rich, but not by violent revolutionary means. 'We have forsworn Revolution for a jog-trot along Social Reform, and there is plenty of time to take things with us on the way – Art above all. . . . Art, if it cannot make men much better as means, can make them very good as ends. To most people it can give something. To some it can give the highest and supremest part of their lives.' The opportunity for the creation of Art, therefore, must be preserved. But if unearned income has been step by step extinguished, who is going to support the artist? Where is the new patron to be found? Rupert answers this crucial problem in some detail and with considerable foresight. He saw that under the old system poets and other creative artists had often not found patronage and had been condemned to extreme poverty. He wanted something less chancy than a 'prince of perfect taste' and immense generosity, a situation that had worked sometimes in the past, in Renaissance Italy for instance. He therefore proposed a National Endowment Committee of about thirty members. 'It could and should be constituted in many different ways, by nomination by the Crown, by, perhaps the Universities, by various official and semi-official bodies such as the Society of Authors, and in other ways – the more irregular the better. You'd get a few stuffy people, no doubt; you'd also get a few creative artists, Thomas Hardy and Yeats, and critics like Professor Sir Walter Raleigh and Mr. Gosse. They would have outer circles of advisers and suggesters. . . .' But the National Endowment Committee, in Rupert's vision, would not be enough by itself. The Universities, the Municipalities, the County Councils should be encouraged to support the arts. And in addition, why not groups of private individuals, not rich enough individually but as a group extremely useful, like the Contemporary Art Society, to support writers and musicians? He thought that the endowments should be for life (as now in New Zealand and Greece) and that £250 per annum would be adequate support for each chosen creative person – the equivalent, I suppose, of more than £3,000 at the time of writing. If all those chosen in every art added up to a thousand persons in all, even that number would only mean an expenditure of a quarter of a million pounds a year, a mere drop in the ocean of a modern budget.

Rupert countered the possible objection that many of those selected for patronage might prove in the end unworthy of it, by saying: 'It is an integral part of the scheme. The choice is between endowing twenty Tuppers to one Byron – and endowing neither.' What he did not face, what he had evidently not conceived in the innocent world of 1910, was that such a State scheme might fall under State political control.

Under Rupert's presidency the Cambridge Fabians flourished vigorously, and became, it was said, the most popular of the political institutions of the University. New premises were opened in Trinity Street, and it boasted 105 members who had signed the Basis, with a further 142 Associates. It had accumulated so many books and pamphlets that it had to appoint a librarian. Rupert had thrown himself into his Fabian activities with the almost feverish zeal that he showed when he espoused any novel cause or scheme, as he had with university theatricals, the founding of the Marlowe Society, and university journalism: he wrote constantly for the *Cambridge Review* and was offered the editorship, which he was wisely advised to decline. He was driven by a desire to excel in everything he touched, to be a leader and be surrounded by an admiring coterie; a temptation difficult to resist for a young man who had become all too well aware of the magnetic attraction he had for almost everyone, of his own or an older generation, male or female, he came into contact with. His circle of friends was continually growing wider, people dropped in on him at all hours of the day or night, and he spent much of his vacations in camps in the country with them, 'dew-dabbling' in true Bedalian fashion. He made constant visits to London, and was much in demand at parties of the most varied sorts. He became a keen playgoer, and was particularly attracted by *Peter Pan* (he had an obsession about staying young), and he had fallen in love with the Court Theatre where he saw several of Shaw's plays. Edward Marsh introduced him into Lady Ottoline Morrell's literary-artistic-political salon in Bedford Square, where he found at least two of the Apostles from Cambridge he already knew, Lytton Strachey and Bertrand Russell. A serious danger was that his health was not really up to the life he was leading, as his frequent breakdowns showed. In his recurring states of utter exhaustion he had no resistance to infection; what was worse was that any small lesion, cut or trifling wound was apt to turn septic and cause a rapidly rising temperature, as if he did not have enough anti-bodies in his bloodstream to cope naturally with them: an ominous condition for the future. During the Long Vacation of 1909, for instance, when Dudley Ward and a crowd of other friends were staying with him and his parents at a house they had rented for the holidays in Clevedon, Somerset, Ward, as they were racing downhill one day, by chance kicked him in the left ankle. 'The hole you made,' Rupert wrote to him afterwards, 'was poisoned by a sock, and, they say, inflamed by tennis; and changed into a sore that grew wider and deeper with incredible rapidity. . . . And I have been on a sofa with my left leg in bandages ever since.'

The sexual tensions of late adolescence may have added to the strain, particularly as he had a strong puritan streak inherited from his mother, and did not, he once said, believe in physical love-making before marriage – though there is some reason to think that he may not have held this belief during his Munich days, and certainly did not allow it to survive the extreme stress of his relations with Ka Cox in 1912, nor the laxer standards of the South Seas. Almost equally serious was that all his social and public activities interfered with his work. He had not done well in his examinations at the end of his first year; but even more alarming for him, and damaging to the image of the brilliant young undergraduate who carried all before him, was that he only got a second in his Tripos at the end of his third year, in May 1909. Rumour went around that some of his examiners thought that he hadn't justified even that rating. He was deeply shocked, and it seems more likely that part of his dismay came from his fear that his mother would be painfully disappointed. He dreaded her disapproval, which was to become extremely outspoken when she began to suspect that he was carrying on an amorous intrigue with one of the Olivier girls; though it seems that she never realized, or found it possible to believe, that though the intrigue did in fact exist it was with the youngest, the schoolgirl Noel.

An odd light is cast on his attitude towards his school-mastering parents by a satirical paper he read to the Carbonari, in Dalton's rooms, in March 1909, which has never been published in full. He invented a character he called John Rump, a caricature of an English middle-class gentleman, repressed, philistine, self-important and unimaginative, and he gave him a schoolmaster father, George Rump, with a wife, Violet, as conventional and contemptible as himself. George Rump's idea of the duties of a housemaster, apart from housing and feeding his charges, was 'to turn a blind eye to sodomy and to prepare the lads for confirmation'. This last phrase is scored out (by whom?), together with an extremely anti-monarchical outburst, in the copy that survives among Rupert's papers. It was, however, quoted by Dalton in the short memoir he sent to Marsh after Rupert's death, though not mentioned by either Marsh or Hassall. There can be little doubt, of course, that no rumour of this paper ever reached his father or mother.

His failure to get a first in his Tripos was a severe blow to his pride. He ate humble pie with his tutor, and readily agreed to his suggestion that for his fourth year he should abandon Classics and turn to English; and, in order to concentrate on his studies more effectively, move not only out of college but out of Cambridge altogether. He took lodgings in Grantchester, a pretty village on the river Granta only a few miles away, but even there the habitual, hectic social round began again. Friends came to spend the afternoon, or the evening, or the week-end; there were boating parties and midnight bathing parties, and streams of letters poured from his pen to absent loved ones who could not always join in. These letters, at any rate from the time he emerged from the early affectations of his letters to St John Lucas until the Lulworth crisis, are flippant, fanciful, facetious, silly, obscene (if one goes to the originals and the unpublished letters), sharp in judgement, intimate, bubbling with ideas, filled with absurd jingles, limericks, parody verses – and always alive. They are written not so much off the top of his head as off the top of his feelings. They give the impression of artless spontaneity, and yet they are nearly always instinctively attuned to the person he is writing to. They are also vividly informative and descriptive of things seen and heard, books read and people encountered. In general, they must have been delightful to receive, though occasionally exasperating.

His closest friends of the earlier years were beginning to scatter : Jacques Raverat was moving to Chelsea; Gwen Darwin, whom he was soon to marry, had become a student at the Slade; Geoffrey Keynes, a student at St Bartholomew's Hospital; James Strachey was acting as secretary to the editor of the *Spectator*, his cousin St Loe Strachey; and Ka was living in York Street, Westminster; nevertheless, with Dudley Ward and Justin and the Olivier sisters, they were continually being re-united at Grantchester or on camping expeditions further afield. Frances Darwin, now married to F. M. Cornford, was still living in Cambridge, and the links between the Cornfords and Rupert grew steadily more intimate. And in the midst of this intense social activity, he was writing poetry all the time, entering for *Westminster Gazette* competitions, and trying to arrange, through various friends, for a first volume of poems to be published. Nor did he lose sight of his prime objective : to make amends for his second in the Tripos. With his indomitable energy he worked hard in every cranny of time left to him. He had entered for the Charles Oldham Shakespeare Scholarship, a distinction that never attracted more than a handful of dedicated enthusiasts every year; and with a first essay on John Webster, the Elizabethan dramatist and poet to whom he had taken a special fancy, succeeded in winning it. A balm to his self-respect, and, what to him was equally important, an earnest to his mother that he was not wasting his time. It also brought the useful addition of £70 in prize money to his always limited funds.

A few months later he entered anonymously for, and won, the Harness Essay Prize, with a study of Puritanism 'as represented or referred to in the early English drama'. By that time (January 1910) his father had died after a long illness, and he had the curious experience of acting as housemaster in his father's place for the first term of the year, while the authorities looked for a replacement at School Field. He missed Cambridge, but he seemed to enjoy the unexpected challenge : he liked order and authority, in spite of John Rump, and he was never at any time an anarchist. His elder brother had died suddenly of pneumonia in 1907, and he was now technically head of the family; but his feeling of subjection to his mother did not change, particularly as he was still dependent on her for his allowance of £150 a year.

His aim for the future was a Fellowship at King's. He was advised that it would be wiser for him to have two shots at it, with a good chance of winning it in 1912–13 if his first shot was sufficiently promising. He set to work, choosing as the subject of his dissertation once more the work of John Webster in the context of the Elizabethan drama. He had already travelled a long way from his adolescent worship of Dowson and Wilde; now the major stars in his poetic firmament, apart from the constellation of the Elizabethan dramatists, were John Milton and, above all, John Donne.

4
Munich and the Old Vicarage

During his fourth year, while he was working for the Shakespeare Scholarship, Rupert lived at a little riverside cottage in Grantchester, known as The Orchard. In December 1910, however, he decided to move to a nearby house, The Old Vicarage, with a large, rambling overgrown garden at the back that led down to the Granta. It was more attractive to him than The Orchard, and the occupants, Mr and Mrs Neeve, were anxious to let off part of the house to a steady lodger in order to augment the very small income they gained from selling honey from their own hives to the trippers and casual tea-time droppers-in from Cambridge. The village had a special charm for Rupert because one could bathe in seclusion there, naked if one wished, in the deep water just above what had come by tradition to be known as Byron's Pool. Shortly before Christmas he moved his books and other belongings from The Orchard and formally began his tenancy; but before he could settle down to working – and entertaining his friends – in the new house, he was off to stay in Munich, as he had long planned, in order to learn German and (one cannot help feeling) to put a greater distance for a while between himself and his mother.

It is clear from his letters from Munich that he often pined for Cambridge and the friends he had left behind. Nevertheless the three months he spent there were a stimulating change for him, though his letters give a persistent picture of him sitting alone in a cafe every evening, drinking hot milk and reading the (day-old) *Times*. He was, however, meeting a number of Germans, both of an older and a younger generation, and sampling their life. He had a letter of introduction to a Professor Schick, a teacher of English, who was to help him learn German; and Schick provided him with a tame student, Ludwig Dellefant, as companion. The idea was that Dellefant should speak English to him and Rupert should reply in German. It didn't always work out that way, but Dellefant introduced him to student societies, where there were discussions, followed by songs (not at all like Lowes Dickinson's serious evenings with the King's College Discussion Society, he noted), and a great deal of beer was consumed. 'The German students,' he told his mother, 'are extremely simple compared with English undergraduates. They are more like very simple, fat, and hearty public-school boys; docile and sentimental.'

He also had a more important introduction from E. J. Dent: to Frau Ewald, a painter, and her son Paul, a student of physics, who had been at Caius for a year. The Ewalds took Rupert under their wing, introduced him to many of their literary and artistic friends, and in particular to Karl Wolfskehl, who had a reputation for befriending young poets and painters. The most interesting thing about Wolfskehl was that he was privileged member of the George Kreis, that group of male devotees who sat at the feet of the famous poet Stefan George, and were inspired by an elevated homosexual worship of beautiful blond youths to whom George wrote his poetry; Rupert, with his pretty schoolboy looks and abundant golden locks could easily have fitted into George's Pantheon, though he was perhaps a little old for it. Wolfskehl conducted a special kind of *salon* in his grand house in the suburb of Schwabing, and on the first Thursday of every month opened his house to the young writers, painters and musicians of the city who had come under his influence. After refreshments, the proceedings grew solemn: lights were turned down, and Wolfskehl would intone the latest poems the Master, Stefan George, had given to the world. It was all very German, and had a touch of that Aryan youth-worship which contributed so strongly to the mystique of National Socialism; though George himself, later on, refused to have anything to do with Hitler.

In one of his letters to James in late January he mentions a comic episode that took place in his lodgings. An Assistant Professor of Physics at Bucharest University, who was also one of the lodgers, was smitten by him. Rupert held him at bay for eight days, but on the Professor's last day, in saying goodbye to him, inadvertently used the familiar 'Du' instead of 'Sie'.

In a flash the Professor's hand went for Rupert's trousers, and he had to flee.

Rupert soon found especial pleasure in the theatrical life of the Bavarian capital, though in the early weeks at least he cannot have understood very much of what was being said on stage. He went to the Opera, to see Richard Strauss's new work, *Der Rosenkavalier*, which was all the rage in Germany at that time, and Wagner's *Ring*. He saw plays by Schnitzler, and as there was an Ibsen festival going on he made a point of seeing every play that was produced. He was especially struck by *John Gabriel Borkman*, preferred it to *The Wild Duck*, and mentions it again and again in his letters. Writing to Jacques Raverat, he remarked: 'Therein is a youth who will fly from his mother in order to LIVE (it happens in Norway also).' It appears that the Ibsen plays were being performed in Dutch, more impenetrable for Rupert than German, but he may have had with him, or been able to obtain, William Archer's English translations.

And then there was Carnival, or *Fasching*, in February, a season of revelry and fancy-dress dances. Rupert threw himself into it with ardour, and enjoyed himself. He went to a *Bacchus Fest*, dressed in Greek classical costume (no doubt a variation on his *Comus* costume as the *Attendant Spirit*). Dawn was breaking as he wandered home. 'There were nine dustmen, me as a Greek, naked and cold, and a crapulous moon. I felt rather tired.' He also records another *Fasching* episode: 'I came late home from a cafe one night, and round the corner of a deserted street came a Pierrot and a Pierrette, a harlequin, a Negress, and a Man in a Top Hat, all in Indian file, stepping in time, very softly, toes pointed, and finger on lip. Whence they came and whither went, I don't know. But it was wonderful.'

Something had happened at the *Bacchus Fest*. He describes how it began in his long letter to Jacques Raverat:

'Then there's me and the sculptress. I don't know what to make of that quite. To begin with, you must know that we have Carnival here in February. Joy. Youth. Flowers. . . . The young lay round in couples, huggin' and kissin'. I roamed around, wondering if I couldn't, once, be even as they, as the animals. I found a round damp young sculptress, a little like Lord Rosebery to look on. We curled passionate limbs round each other in a perfuctory manner and lay in a corner, sipping each other and beer in polite alternation. . . . We roamed and sat and even danced and lay and talked, and the night wore on. We became more devoted. My head was in her lap, she was munching my fingers, when suddenly I became quite coldly aware of my position in the Universe. "I, M. or N., who knows – and – and" . . . the whole thing came to me. I knew there was a Crisis at hand. I turned and said "My dear Lady Rosebery, this is the Grand Climacteric. By the shaking of your enormous melancholy mouth I see that is also true for you. I haven't the dimmest idea what sort of a Grand Climacteric a Dutch sculptress has: but I may as well say, frankly, now, that, though I'm really a long way beyond Greece, and I find the point of things distinctly elsewhere, and I demand more especially that keen mixture of intimacy and sensuality, body and brain, which Cupid has given us now that we moderns have unblindfolded him, yet, since, even if *one*'s a bit intellectual, it's all right so long as the *other* of the pair – you in fine – is happy, I am, my dear, quite ready . . . eager . . . to – to put it colloquially – 'go on'!." But then we put hands on each others' necks and shoulders for the millionth time and found them quite cool, and she raised her watery protruding eyes to mine, and I suddenly realized of her – and she of me – that she was in exactly the same state, that she, too, was trying Greece, was quite a conscious, sensible intellectual, real, modern person – might, in fact, in other circumstances, have been almost, not quite, one of Us – "we found", in short – to quote one quite admirable sonnet I wrote on the whole thing next afternoon – "that *we*,

   Were *you* (whoever *you* may be!) and I!"

And as one can't very well begin a new game at five in the morning, we very solemnly and pathetically kissed each other on our quiet intellectual lips and so parted. . . .'

Who was this 'Dutch sculptress'? We are not told in this letter; but in Munich, just at this time, a certain Elizabeth Van Rysselberghe entered his life. She was the daughter of a Belgian Impressionist painter – the name is obviously Flemish, which is hardly to be distinguished from Dutch – and was seven years older than Rupert. She is mentioned in a letter written about the same time to Geoffrey Keynes: 'My life in Munchen isn't wildly thrilling. I don't emulate Dudley with women. I sit alone in a cafe or my room and read or write.... Of course there's Elizabeth.... But then there's always somebody.... But there's never anybody *quite* like Elizabeth.... Oh! Oh! But as she's spoilt my life, and given me a devilish cold in the head, but let's pass to pleasanter topics.' He mentions her several times in his letters to James Strachey, and in one letter at the end of April 1911 he describes an extremely painful scene of parting with Elizabeth when he left Munich: she became, he writes, completely distraught, weeping on the sofa with her hair down, while he stood awkwardly beside her, trying to explain why he was leaving and feeling like an awful snake. She appears again as the young woman who helped him across Paris in the crisis of 1912. 'Elizabeth was very kind,' he wrote to Ka on that January day,

'and waited some eighty minutes for my late train, and packed me into a cab. She has gone out to telegraph, and reserve me seats, and change me money. I sit by the fire and read the original MSS of Mon. Verhaeren and Gide. I'm glad I didn't go straight on. To get as far as this was sufficiently tiring. I'm only a little cross that I'm in a way imposing on Elizabeth. I find myself so unmoved and kindly with her. All the passion I had once and the horrible mixture of lust and dislike I had at another time are gone so far away. I'm only tiredly well-meaning and slightly responsible.'

And he adds, a little later in the letter, 'Don't mind my being here a day. I'm not loving Elizabeth.'

It is difficult to resist the conclusion that the Dutch sculptress met at the *Bacchus Fest* and Elizabeth Van Rysselberghe were one and the same person; though until further documents are available we cannot be absolutely certain. Nevertheless it seems clear from all the evidence that an affair developed between Elizabeth and Rupert, perhaps the first consummated love affair with a woman in his life. She is only given a brief mention on one page of Christopher Hassall's biography – in connection with the night in Paris – but we know that in one of his last letters from the *Grantully Castle* in March 1915 Rupert asks Dudley Ward to destroy all her letters; and that in after years she maintained that she had been his mistress, and wished that she had had a child by him. She did have a child by André Gide, his daughter Catherine.

At the beginning of April, after three months in Munich, Rupert left for Vienna, where he joined an old Cambridge friend, also a Fabian, E. P. Goldschmidt, whom he described as 'a very rich and clever Jew who used to be at Trinity'. He seems to have on the whole enjoyed his time in Munich – 'I was infinitely lethargic but contented there,' he wrote to Dent, and was deeply grateful for all that had been done for him by Frau Ewald 'my mother and all my aunts'; but departed with a distinctly unfavourable view of Germany and German culture. He wrote to Marsh:

> 'It has changed all my political views. I am wildly in favour of nineteen new Dreadnoughts. German culture must never, never prevail. The German are nice, & well-meaning, & they try; but they are SOFT. Oh! They ARE soft. The only good things (outside music perhaps) are the writings of Jews who live in Vienna. Have you heard of Mr. Schnitzler's historical play [Der Junge Medarhus]? They act an abbreviated version which lasts from 7 to 12. I saw it. A Hebrew journalist's version of *The Dynasts*; but rather good.'

He had intended to go on a walking tour in Dalmatia with Goldschmidt, but he suddenly learned that his younger brother Alfred was on his way to Florence, escorting his old schoolmaster and godfather, Robert Whitelaw, who had recently lost his wife and was too old to travel alone. Alfred could only accompany him on the outward journey; so Rupert volunteered to be with him in Florence and take him back. It was a nostalgic episode: they indulged in many reminiscences of the past, while they visited galleries and churches. Rupert thought that the people in the pension where he stayed, English clergymen, their wives and spinster relatives, were 'all Forster characters. Perhaps it is *his* pension. But to live among Forster characters is too bewildering. The "quaint" remarks fall all round one at meal-time, with little soft plups like pats of butter.'

Early in May 1911 he took Whitelaw back to Rugby, and then left to start his new life at the Old Vicarage. It was one of his happiest summers. In July he wrote to Ka: 'There is no wind and no sun, only a sort of warm haze, and through it the mingled country sounds of a bee, a mowing machine, a mill and a sparrow. Peace! And the content of working all day at Webster. Reading and reading and reading. It's not noble, but it's so happy. Oh, *come* here!' And at the end of summer, in September, he wrote to his cousin Erica : 'All the Spring I lived in Germany & learnt strange things. All the summer I alternated between seeing the Russian Ballet at Covent Garden [he made 15 visits] and writing sonnets on the lawn here. This is a deserted, lonely, dank, ruined, overgrown, gloomy, lovely house : with a garden to match. It is all five hundred years old, and fusty with the ghosts of generations of mouldering clergymen.'

He certainly worked harder and less interruptedly during this summer of 1911 than he had the year before; but the entertaining of friends and other visitors went on, if rather less feverishly. One of the visitors that came to the Old Vicarage was Virginia Stephen, to whom he seems to have become especially attached. Long before, as I have already mentioned, when he was only six and she was eleven, he and his brother Dick had played cricket with her at St Ives, where she acquired the nickname of 'the demon bowler'. There is a passage in one of his letters to James Strachey in 1910, in which he describes having come across two photographs of about 1893, which showed himself and his brother Dick at St Ives with the Stephen family : Thoby, Vanessa, Virginia, Adrian, and their father Sir Leslie, 'all very sporting and odd' in which Virginia looked a little gawky and decidedly fat-faced. He had almost certainly met her again as early as 1908 or 1909, either through Lytton or James, or perhaps when she stayed with the Darwins at Newnham Grange. She was already by then contributing book reviews and essays to the *Times Literary Supplement* and other papers; she may have been writing one of them while she was staying with Rupert, or have been at work on an early draft of her first novel *The Voyage Out*, which was published in 1915 (Rupert heard from Marsh of its appearance just before his death in the Aegean) but had taken her five or six years to complete. One warm, moonlit night during her 1911 visit they went for a walk, following the stream to Byron's pool, and on a sudden impulse Rupert said: 'Let's go swimming quite naked' – and Virginia plunged in with him. She was, we are told, disappointed that when she related this act of daring to her Bloomsbury friends it did not cause more of a sensation; though it may

have been one of the episodes which caused Bloomsbury to give
Rupert and his friends the nickname of 'Neo-Pagans'.

Another visitor that summer from the precincts of Bloomsbury was David Garnett, whom Rupert joined again shortly
afterwards for a week's sailing on the Broads, with Margery
and Brynhild Olivier. They had met briefly the year before at
a camp at Penshurst. At the Old Vicarage David Garnett noted
that:

> 'The Old Vicarage garden was unkempt and trailed off into
> an orchard with overhanging trees by the water and a little
> summerhouse, derelict under them, with paintings by Duncan
> Grant in it. . . . One of the first things I noticed in the Old
> Vicarage was a photograph of Noel in a silver frame on the
> table. I did not remark on it, neither did Rupert mention her.
> Rupert could not have been more delightful. He was quite
> free from airs of superiority, which it must have been difficult
> to avoid with such a half-baked creature as myself. And he
> was quite free, also, from any affectations such as I noticed
> later. Instead, he was easy and kind, hospitable and yet
> happily pre-occupied with his own work.
>
> We went about midnight – for I had arrived rather late – to
> bathe in Byron's Pool. We walked out of the garden of the
> Old Vicarage into the lane full of thick white dust, which
> slipped under our weight as we walked noiselessly in our
> sand-shoes, and then through the dew-soaked grass of the
> meadow over the mill-wall leading to the pool, to bathe naked
> in the unseen water, smelling of wild peppermint and mud.'

Of the holiday on the Broads, David Garnett (who was five
years younger than Rupert) wrote: 'I was very happy and
was aware that for some reason Rupert liked me. That holiday
was the time of my closest friendship with him. His immense
charm and intelligence had not yet been spoilt by success and
by certain *idées fixes*, which later came to resemble hallucina-
tions. With me, in our midnight cabin talks, he was simple,
sincere and intimate, with a certain lazy warmth. It was only
later that he was apt to utter warnings about the wickedness
of other people.'

Sybil Pye, artist and bookbinder, whose family lived close
to the Oliviers at Limpsfield, and whose general impression of
Rupert I have already quoted, was also a visitor to Grantchester

that summer. 'It was interesting to see,' she wrote in her fondly nostalgic article in *Life and Letters* (May 1929),

'so strong a sense as his for ordinary, practical life. The constant small decisions required to run a day's machinery were never allowed to become with him the burden they so often are to people of wide imagination. In one of our discussions, the phrase "an artistic eye in a business head" caught his attention; he said he believed the combination *was* possible, and he certainly aimed at making it so. I think there is no doubt he had a happy talent for organization, and that he combined it with social gifts really surprising in one of his naturally shy temperament. These powers were conspicuous on one occasion at Grantchester, when three separate May Week parties, falling on the same date and anxious not to deprive each other of guests, combined to meet in our garden. Among the mutual acquaintances, there seemed a large number of people strange to each other, and having little clue to the tastes and outlook of the company as a whole; and the task of combining such diverse elements into one easy and sympathetic social body, appeared, to an onlooker, barely worth the attempt. Rupert, however, thought otherwise – or, rather, I do not believe he thought at all – he just moved from group to group, dissolving incongruities and creating links. . . .

On some days he would take an armful of books into a canoe, and keeping a paddle in his left hand to steady it while the current drifted him along, would make rapid notes on scraps of paper from one book and another, and, in an easy mood, read out passages to enjoy the sound of the various forms and cadences. Spenser, Ben Jonson, Beaumont and Fletcher, Webster and many lesser-known song-writers of their time – all these keep an added gracious quality for those who heard them in this manner, among the dark reflected trees and the sudden wide openings across flat misty meadows. . . .

The affection he felt for this river is already familiar to readers of his poems. Each curve of its course, and each tree-clump that marked it, seemed known to him with a peculiar intimacy – like that which attaches sometimes to things constantly and affectionately handled. Coming up

with him in a canoe those three miles from Cambridge to
Grantchester, on a dark, starless night, this knowledge was
sufficiently startling to one possessing no clue to it. Every
possible landmark seemed merged in a soft blackness; even
the water-surface had ceased to show the faintest gleam,
and met its muffled banks invisibly. Except for the low sound
of the paddles, we might have been floating in some new
medium, without boundaries and out of reach of light – of
time, too, perhaps. But Rupert kept a steady course; he would
know, he said, when we were nearing home, by the sound of
a certain poplar tree that grew there : its leaves rustled faintly
even on such nights as this, when not a breath seemed
stirring. We only half believed him; there were so many
poplar trees by that river, and it sounded absurd to recognize
the voice of one. But he was right; and he landed us without
hesitation, and moored his boat as easily, it seemed, as if he
had all the light of day to help him.'

With so many of his earlier Cambridge friends dispersed by
the time he was lodging at the Old Vicarage, he began to grow
even closer to the Cornfords, living during all this time at
Conduit Head, and particularly to Frances, fellow-poet, confidante, and affectionate but shrewd observer : of all his friends
perhaps she was the one who understood him best. They read
their poems to one another, with critical judgements freely
expressed : he sometimes complained that her lyrics were just
the 'old, old heart-cry business', and she objected that there
was too much of the 'over-grand' manner about his work. She
thought – though she probably didn't tell him so to his face –
that, at that time at least, though he worked at his effects with
the most deliberate artifice, and was in fact the most con-
scientious of craftsmen, he very seldom seemed to have the
sudden spontaneous inspiration of a line or phrase. In later
years, after his death, she endeavoured to give an essential
impression of him as he appeared to her then :

'It was a continual pleasure to look at him fresh each day –
his radiant fairness, beauty of build, his broad head with its
flung-back hair, deep-set frowning eyes. The clear line of his
chin and long broad-based neck on broad shoulders were so
entirely beautiful that he seemed like a symbol of youth for
all time. . . . To watch him putting on his boots, frowning

and groaning, with the absorbed seriousness of a child, with which he did all practical things – he would look up with a pink face and his pleasant hair tumbled and his sudden sharing grin which always had the loveliness of a child.'

She noted the strong strain of puritanism in his make-up, an element that was to cause such havoc in the aftermath of the Lulworth crisis: 'Deep ingrained in him, and handed down to him I should imagine through generations of English ancestors, was the puritanical spirit. I remember how clearly it showed when he spoke the Chorus in *Faustus* in some sort of Puritan scholar's dress. And nobody could miss it, who ever saw the scorn and sternness in his face when he spoke of things that he hated, things corrupt and unclean.' Unclean, cleanness – these words kept on recurring in his letters and poems: Frances Cornford had put her finger on a sensitive spot, a shockable, anti-sensual side to his character that emotional misfortune only hardened.

She also noted that he was distinctly conscious of his 'pretty schoolboy' looks. Sybil Pye maintains that he was totally un-selfconscious, but one cannot read his youthful letters or study the early portrait photographs of him without being aware of a conscious underlying impulse to pose. When Frances Cornford heard that he had just met Henry James, she said to him 'So of course you were frank and boyish?' 'Oh yes,' he replied (she tells us), 'of course I did the fresh, boyish stunt, and it was a great success.'

In the absence of access to the letters which he almost certainly, in spite of all technical difficulties, had been writing to Noel Olivier since their secret engagement at Buckler's Hard in 1910, it is difficult to know how his relationship with her was progressing. We do know, however, that he was beginning to suspect that her eldest sister Margery's watchful guardianship while the parents were away in Jamaica was perhaps less disinterested than he had at first thought. Was she jealous? He went as far as to write to Ka that he had at moments believed her to be wicked. 'Not very judicially, but I do. And what's to be done if you think a person you know so well is wicked?' Then early in January 1911 he went to stay at the Oliviers' home at Limpsfield, when he obviously accused Margery of causing unnecessary obstruction between himself and Noel. Margery denied it, Noel supported her. He apologized; felt guilty; but at the same time began to be aware of an emotional confusion that he couldn't quite analyse or control.

He told Ka all this. She seems to have completely accepted Noel's priority in Rupert's affections; but she must nevertheless have been half aware that one of the causes of the emotional confusion was her almost imperceptibly changing relationship with him. He comforted her in her bitter disappointment over Jacques Raverat's engagement and marriage to Gwen Darwin; she comforted him and counselled calm and patience in his situation with Noel; but it began to seem as if he needed more comfort than she did, and sudden moments of tension between them hinted that their relationship was beginning to be just a little overcharged with emotion. There was an incident over a Christmas present when they were together in a bookshop; his apparently off-hand attitude seemed to her to suggest that he didn't care what book she gave him – it was all one to him. She was hurt; he realized too late that he had been callous and cruel; bitter recriminations followed. Then there was the incident at the station on his departure for Munich : he suddenly found he couldn't say goodbye to her affectionately, and walked away abruptly to his compartment. He was afraid, he admitted later, that too much emotion would well up; he was desperately ashamed of having hurt her. Once in Munich, he wrote to her that he longed for her to join him. Later, in July, at the Old Vicarage, he wrote her a telling letter : 'Oh, why do you invite responsibilities? Are you a Cushion, or a Floor? Ignoble thought! But why does your face invite one to load weariness on you? Why does your body appeal for an extra load of responsibilities? . . . Oh, but I want to see you. Just now I'm scribbling this merely to say that I think you're a most lovely and splendid and superb and loved person.' Soon after this, she came at last to stay at the Old Vicarage, with a room on the other side of the house. Something in the way they behaved when they were together, perhaps in the way they talked about one another to their friends, aroused surmises in those quick to notice such things. Not long after her visit, he suddenly wrote to her while he was staying with his mother in Rugby for a few days : 'Ka, they've been Talking, about You and Me. Talking! Awful. If you only knew what James said Virginia said So and So said . . . ! These mediate ignorances! But your repper, my dear, is going.

Oh, among the quite Advanced. I, it is thought, am rather beastly; you rather pitiable. How otherwise, you see, can a situation be explained when two people have, in no *Morning Post*, "arranged a marriage"? Isn't it too monstrous? They gibber night and morning, teleologically. "How will it end?" They impudently ache for us. . . . We will talk. Do not fret. That's hardly worth the saying. We are covered from sight by a blazing veil of rightness.' The news that Dudley Ward was going to be married, to a German girl called Annemarie, increased his feeling of being left behind: first Frances, then Gwen and Jacques, and now Dudley. He felt more dependent than ever on Ka's sympathy and understanding; but he was worried that – so rumour reached him – she was being seen about town rather too frequently with the young painter he had met at Lady Ottoline's, Henry Lamb.

Such was the state of affairs when he went to join his mother at Eastbourne, and then went home with her to Rugby for Christmas. He had high hopes that the reading party he was organizing for the New Year at Lulworth would rest and refresh him: the dissertation in its first shape was at last finished. Ka would be with him, and many of his oldest friends would be gathered round. In addition, his first book of poems had at last been published: surely a moment for great pride and satisfaction in a young poet's life.

What actually happened at Lulworth I have already related.

5
Poems 1911

Rupert had been working slowly and carefully towards his first book of poems ever since he began his life as an undergraduate at Cambridge. Before that, however, in his final year at Rugby, he had won his first public recognition (and his first cheque – for 10s 6d) in a competition set by the *Westminster Gazette*, a weekly journal edited by the well-known journalist J. A. Spender, with a regular competition page under the direction of Naomi Royde Smith. The instructions for the entries were often extremely precise, and would seem to have stimulated Rupert's muse by their challenge. The poem by which he won his prize was written in answer to specifications set out for 'a Sonnet entitled The Sea'. It is of little or no importance in Rupert's work, but it encouraged him, and started a regular habit of entering for the competitions, which undoubtedly developed his craftsmanship and his capacity to find his own voice. It even provided an addition to his finances, small but not to be sniffed at for a young man living on an annual allowance of £150. In the spring of 1909 he won four prizes in succession. What is of significance in these verses is that they showed that he had a distinct gift for parody and light verse with a flavour of nonsense.

While at King's he contributed a number of poems to Cambridge magazines, and had begun to send them further afield: in the September 1909 issue of the *English Review* four poems of his appeared, which were all included in his first book (*The Life Beyond, Blue Evening, Sleeping Out*, and *The Song of the Beasts*). The idea for a volume started hazily to take shape. His friend Jacques Raverat suggested arranging to have them privately printed by a firm he knew in London; but when he told Frances Cornford she immediately advised him to avoid a private printing – there was 'a touch of preciousness' about it, she said. He realized that it was sensible advice, and decided to discourage Raverat. He also realized that the volume would still be very slim indeed. Two more years passed before he made a serious approach to a publisher, by which time he had added a number of new poems which he was confident strengthened the collection.

Poems 1911 was published by Sidgwick and Jackson at the beginning of December 1911. He had offered the dedication to Noel, but when she refused, thinking it wiser still to keep their intimacy a secret, he left the book without any dedication. The costs, which amounted to £9 17s 6d, were paid for by Rupert himself, or rather by his mother; before the end of the year that sum had already been covered by sales, and it was showing a profit of nearly £3. It is ironical to note that in the following twenty years 37 impressions were printed, amounting to all but 100,000 copies. Sidgwick and Jackson were eventually to make a huge profit by the venture which they had entered into with much hesitation and commercial doubt.

There had been difficulties between them and the author about the choice of poems to be included. Rupert showed himself to be fairly tough – or at least he put on a show of being tough – in his negotiations on this matter. For some time he had been in process of shedding the skin of shallow ninetyish affectation of diction and subject matter, which he had acquired largely under the influence of St John Lucas, and searching for an anti-romantic realism of both manner and content. One can suggest that this was partly due to his deepening admiration for Donne, and his approval of the frequent 'coarseness' of his beloved Elizabethan dramatists, partly to his study of the crude facts of the life of the poor in his Fabian phase, and partly because such a change was 'in the air', as the brief Edwardian period drew to its close – John Masefield's *Everlasting Mercy* was also published in 1911. One of the early results of this process of change was a sonnet originally entitled *Lust*:

> How should I know? The enormous wheels of will
> Drove me cold-eyed on tired and sleepless feet.
> Night was void arms and you a phantom still,
> And day your far light swaying down the street.

As never fool for love, I starved for you;
My throat was dry and my eyes hot to see.
Your mouth so lying was most heaven in view,
And your remembered smell most agony.
Love wakens love! I felt your hot wrist shiver
And suddenly the mad victory I planned
Flashed real, in your burning bending head. . . .
My conqueror's blood was cool as a deep river
In shadow; and my heart beneath your hand
Quieter than a dead man on a bed.

This innocuous piece of work, added at the last moment, was too much for Frank Sidgwick. 'We think we must ask you to omit it.' Rupert reacted strongly. 'If it's thought to be improper it must be sadly misunderstood. Its meaning is quite "proper" and so moral as to be almost untrue. . . . My own feeling is that to remove it would be to overbalance the book still more in the direction of unimportant prettiness. There's plenty of that sort of wash in the other pages for the readers who like it.' In the end Sidgwick agreed to its inclusion, but under the substitute title Rupert proposed of *Libido* – which removed a nasty crude Anglo-Saxon word, but otherwise changed nothing.

When his older friend and devotee, Edward Marsh, to whom he had shown many of the poems as he finished them, first read the book, his objection to the retitled sonnet was the word 'smell'. 'There are some things too disgusting to write about, especially in one's own language.' This astonishing maiden-lady-ish reaction puzzled Rupert. 'The "smell" business I don't really understand. . . . People do smell other people, as well as see and feel them. I do, and I'm not disgusted to think so.' However, Marsh's letter was so full of heart-warming praise that he couldn't be angry over an objection of detail. Marsh had written: 'I had always in trembling hope reposed that I should like the poems, but at my wildest I never looked forward to such magnificence. . . . You have brought back into English poetry the rapturous beautiful grotesque of the 17th century.' Bravely, he swallowed his other objection: 'The *Channel Passage* is so clever and amusing that in spite of a prejudice in favour of poetry that I can read at meals I can't wish it away.'

A Channel Passage caused so much trouble with the critics that it must also be quoted in full:

The damned ship lurched and slithered. Quiet and quick
My cold gorge rose; the long sea rolled; I knew
I must think hard of something, or be sick;
And could think hard of only one thing – *you*
You, you alone could hold my fancy ever!
And with you memories come, sharp pain and dole.
Now there's a choice – heartache or tortured liver!
A sea-sick body, or a you-sick soul!
Do I forget you? Retchings twist and tie me,
Old meat, good meals, brown gobbets, up I throw.
Do I remember? Acrid return and slimy,
The sobs and slobber of a last year's woe.
And still the sick ship rolls. 'Tis hard, I tell ye,
To choose 'twixt love and nausea, heart and belly.

One can look at this sonnet as an amusing and skilful exercise
of Rupert's talent for light verse; it can hardly be considered
more. If it was meant to shock, it succeeded. Most reviewers
failed to notice the tongue in the cheek, the impish spirit at
work; from their reactions one might think he had crudely
described the act of sexual intercourse. 'What possible excuse,'
wrote the *Morning Post*, 'is there for a sonnet describing a rough
Channel crossing with gusto worthy of a medical dictionary?'
The *New Age* agreed: 'The appalling narrative of a cross-
Channel voyage should never have been included in the volume.
It spreads its aroma all round.' Observing the use of the word
'aroma' in this particular context, Rupert may have smiled to
note that 'smell' was taboo in polite reviewing also, even
describing something that disgusted the reviewer. There were
plenty of other reviews in the same vein, but the *Times Literary
Supplement* took a slightly different line about it: 'His disgusting sonnet on love and sea-sickness ought never to have
been printed; but we are tempted to like him for writing it.
Most people pass through some such strange nausea as this on
their stormy way from romance to reality ... here is clearly a
rich nature – sensuous, eager, brave – fighting eagerly towards
the truth.' Once the critics had got over *A Channel Passage*, in
fact, the more percipient among them saw that an original
and accomplished poetic talent had made its debut. John Buchan
in the *Spectator* called it 'a book of rare and remarkable
promise'; the *English Review* recommended it to 'any reader

who was capable of being charmed by melody and amused by
the ironic imagination'. Most authors would, I think, agree that
the sharpest criticism often comes from quarters one would
expect to be favourable; and the *Westminster Gazette*, in the
pages of which he had already made so many star appearances,
thought that he ought to find 'the courage to be less startlingly
unusual in the future', and on the subject of the 'disgusting
sonnet' made the astonishing observation that 'the bravest,
purest soul that ever saw no harm would be forced to wince
before such a remorseless catalogue of ignoble symptoms'. It
did, however, give him a pat on the back, promising him an
'enduring place in the future' if only he wouldn't do it again.
Rupert must have taken more heart from the judgement of his
friend Edward Thomas (who had not yet written a single poem),
given in the *Daily Chronicle* a few months later : 'He is full of
revolt, contempt, self-contempt, and yet arrogance too. He
reveals chiefly what he desires to be and to be thought. . . .
Copies should be bought by everyone over forty who has never
been under forty. It will be a revelation. And if they live yet a
little longer they may see Mr. Rupert Brooke a poet. He will
not be a little one.'

Another poem, which aroused a certain tetchiness of unease
in some of the older critics, was his second sonnet on *Menelaus
and Helen*. In the first he had imagined how Menelaus had
discovered Helen when he broke into Priam's palace 'sword in
hand', and promptly fallen in love with her, 'the perfect Knight
before the perfect Queen'. In the second, adopting a sharply
contrasting anti-romantic tone, he had written :

> So far the poet. How should he behold
> That journey home, the long connubial years ?
> He does not tell you how white Helen bears
> Child on legitimate child, becomes a scold,
> Haggard with virtue. Menelaus bold
> Waxed garrulous, and sacked a hundred Troys
> 'Twixt noon and supper. And her golden voice
> Got shrill as he grew deafer. And both were old.
>
> Often he wonders why on earth he went
> Troyward, or why poor Paris ever came.
> Oft she weeps, gummy-eyed and impotent;
> Her dry shanks twitch at Paris' mumbled name.

> So Menelaus nagged; and Helen cried;
> And Paris slept on by Scamander side.

This was hardly more caustically realistic than Shakespeare had been in *Troilus and Cressida*; but the dissenting critics felt that it was definitely not good taste in 1911. *Jealousy*, written about the same time, embodies the same mood.

One can see that as Rupert moved out of his cloudily ardent romanticism with its Swinburnian echoes, the influences and ideals that were beginning to make themselves felt were very much in tune with the new spirit in poetry. *Channel Passage* is not far in tone from the more scurrilously light-hearted and disillusioned asides in Byron's *Don Juan*. Some reviewers had indeed noted an element of Byronism; only the writer in the *Morning Post* noted the influence of Browning. Rupert had long been an admirer, and two years later, in an article published only in a German magazine, declared his admiration and the reasons for it: 'He showed his audience romance, not in wistful, remote, imaginary ages or people, but in the characters of such cheats, imposters, failures and heroes as they saw about them. And he did this in no artificial, brocaded "poet's" language, but with all the colloquialisms of ordinary life enriched by a thousand rarities and grotesqueries of his own collecting.' He also noted the curious fact that the most direct descendants of Browning, those who had hitherto showed the mark of his mind and manner most clearly, were not poets but prose writers (an observation which may call to mind Oscar Wilde's witticism, in *The Critic as Artist*, that 'Meredith is a prose Browning, and so is Browning').

Above all, the cool intellectual spirit of Donne was beginning to show itself in the more maturely successful poems written after 1908, such as *Mummia*. In spite of the still unexorcised ghost of sloppy romanticism that filled the poems with exclamations about the 'holy joy' he had in contemplating his imaginary love, the 'light of laughter' (there is a great deal of joyous carefree laughter ringing through the volume), the 'changing faces that I loved' that moved 'proud in their careless transience' and such embarrassing lines as 'Love so from earth to ecstacies unwist', he already knew where he wanted to go, if he could only as yet move uncertainly in the desired direction.

The watershed appears to be somewhere between 1908 and

1909. When the collected *Poetical Works* was published in 1946 his shrewdest, though deeply admiring, critic, Frances Cornford, wrote in *Time and Tide* regretting the number of poems of the earlier period which had been added: 'These early pieces show little more than adolescent, poetic emotion, and the determination of a most serious and scholarly apprentice to master the full orchestration of the English language. A very little of his early work is quite enough to show how gifted he was from the beginning, and how much skill he had learnt from Belloc, Housman, Dowson and the "decadent" poets of the nineties. But these were, on the whole, dangerous influences – he was far too apt to absorb not only their skill but their mannerisms.' She went on to complain that his 'sad mournful roses, flesh more fair than pale lilies, his ultimate sad breaths, grey-eyed lute-players, and all the rest of it' were 'damaging to Brooke's reputation for sincerity, not to say humour'. 'Could any educated reader or writer want any more of this sort of thing? Because I still take Rupert Brooke seriously as a poet, these, and many other verbal affectations which he never wholly outgrew, still make me blush painfully.'

The distance he had already travelled before the war broke out is clearly shown by the difference between the rather lush romantic diction of his first fish poem (early 1911) included in this book, and the perfectly controlled wit and irony of the second, *Heaven*, written in 1913.

All in all, Rupert's first volume had made its mark. The critics would not have bothered even to be shocked if they had not been, in one way or another, impressed by the promise that so eloquently manifested itself, for all the uncertainty of tone and immaturity of feeling, in vigour of mind and imagination in so many of the poems.

Part Two

6

London and the Georgians

The new world of friends into whose orbit Rupert was drawn after his emotional crisis over Ka, came to him through another Apostle he had met in Cambridge days, Edward Marsh, known as Eddie to his friends, a civil servant who was later knighted. His response to Rupert's *Poems 1911* I have already quoted. He was a bachelor, a collector of poets and young painters. He had been in Cambridge to see the performance of the *Eumenides* of Aeschylus in the Michaelmas term of 1908. Rupert, a freshman, was, as I have already described, playing the very small part of the Herald; but Marsh was captivated by him on the spot. He made a point of cultivating his acquaintance at subsequent meetings of the Apostles. By the spring of 1909 their friendship had developed so far that he invited Rupert, whenever he visited London, to stay with him in his chambers at Raymond's Buildings, Gray's Inn. In the course of the next few years this became a home from home for Rupert, in fact his regular address in London. At the same time he began to write long and detailed letters to Marsh, which are one of the most important biographical sources for the last phase of Rupert's life; though it seems unlikely that he confided to him the torments he went through over the affair with Ka.

Marsh was working in the Colonial Office when they first met; but by the time Rupert had published his first book of poems in 1911, he had become Secretary to the First Lord of the Admiralty, Winston Churchill, still at that time a member of the Liberal Party and one of its most outstanding figures. By virtue of this privileged position, he had the entrée to the social set in which Winston was a leading light; brilliant, cultivated, well-read people of money and influence, but more interested in politics and power than in intellectual matters and certainly at a far remove from Bloomsbury. It was inevitable that Marsh's new protégé, in reaction against his former bohemian friends, but with all the fascination of his looks and rising poetic reputation about him, and a Fellowship of King's in the offing, should be drawn into their orbit.

For the time being, however, Marsh and Rupert were becoming involved in an exciting poetic enterprise. The date was September 1912. In the course of a discussion with Rupert one evening, Marsh, who followed new developments in poetry very closely, maintained that in spite of Rupert's doubts a new spirit was stirring and that he could name at least a dozen living poets, several of them scarcely known at all, who, if grouped together, would show the public just that. The idea caught Rupert's fancy, and the very next day the two of them started planning an anthology, for which Harold Monro's newly born Poetry Bookshop was to be the publishing channel. They began to gather in the poets at once.

Rupert had already got to know James Elroy Flecker at Cambridge, where they had overlapped. Flecker, three years older than Rupert, had been an undergraduate at Trinity College, Oxford, and had subsequently arrived at Caius College early in 1908, as an advanced student of Oriental languages, with the intention of joining the Consular service. They do not appear to have hit it off particularly happily together, but they clearly met and discussed poetry together on many occasions, and showed one another the poems they were writing. On one occasion Flecker wrote to him as 'your brother in poesy' and claimed to see him as 'our Donne Redivivus'. He had published his first book of poems, *The Bridge of Fire*, in 1907; his second book appeared a few years later, and received a rather grudging and patronizing review from Rupert (by that time Flecker had left Cambridge). He ended, however, with a modicum of praise: 'Mr. Flecker too often seems to have been inspired with a few good lines, and completed the poems with a few dull ones. . . . Luckily, the few good lines always make the poem worth it. How good, then, the various unspoilt poems! The feeling in them is not of the strong, true English kind, that starved and morbid young men think they have, sometimes, not (in Mr. Flecker's own words) "the strong man's joy, refined and cold", but the healthy human man's vulgar and mixed emotions, made, somehow, beautiful by the magic of poetry.' The poems so strongly tinged with an Oriental exoticism that made an immediate appeal to contemporary taste, were still in the making. Rupert, incidentally, thought that Flecker had been guilty of 'a more serious, moral fault' in calling one of his best-known poems *The Queen's Song*. Whatever the rather obscure fault was (the ambiguous meaning of Queen – in 1910?), it went into *Georgian Poetry*.

Only one letter to him from Rupert survives, written in 1912, when Flecker had already entered the Consular service and had been posted to Beirut, in which Rupert tells him about his breakdowns:

'I, as another poet once, have fallen on the thorns of life and bled bucketsful. And I am far too poor to give you the copy of my poems you indecently ask for. . . . Oh yes, the Crash came. Precisely at the beginning of this year. I galloped down hill for months and then took the abysm with a leap, like Decimus Somebody. Nine days I lay without sleep or food. Monsters of the darkest Hell nibbled my soul. They nibbled it away and therein that noblest part of it which men name the intellect. I am sodden and soft and dead. . . . My swarthy friend Elroy, my golden-tongued and lax-metred Orpheus, you would never let me teach you how to write Poetry; but it does not matter now: and you are a fine fellow. . . .'

When Flecker died of consumption at Davos in January 1915 Rupert wrote the obituary for him which appeared in *The Times*.

John Masefield he had met at least by the summer of 1912, that is a month or two before the evening when the idea of *Georgian Poetry* was born. He went to stay with him in his cottage at Great Hampden, and described him as 'singing old sea-shanties to the baby' inside, while he himself sat outside writing poetry. John Masefield had already published *Salt Water Ballads* (in which the famous *Sea Fever* appeared) several years before Rupert made his acquaintance, and *Ballads and Poems* (with the equally much-anthologized *Cargoes*) in 1910. The long narrative poem *The Everlasting Mercy* appeared at the same time as Rupert's *Poems 1911*, and at once caught the fancy of the poetry-reading public. Edward Davison wrote, many years later, that it 'called a new tune which set the muse dancing, not very classically, in full view of the man in the street for the first time since the days of Tennyson.' In his earlier ballads Masefield had shown himself to be in the tradition of Kipling, and might be said to be doing for the world of men serving under the Red Duster what Kipling had done for the world of Tommy Atkins. They should have prepared the public for the realism of *The Everlasting Mercy* (as Robert Ross observes in *The Georgian Revolt*), but it startled and surprised and, what was more, could be appreciated without the benefit of a classical education. 'Its modernity,' wrote Harold Monro, 'its bald colloquialism, and its narrative interest awakened the curiosity of the public in 1911, and a revival of the dormant interest in poetry was at once assured.' It was natural that Masefield and Rupert should find much in common in their views about the direction poetry should take.

On the evening before their crucial discussion, he and Marsh had picked up Wilfred Gibson, a poet who had recently come down south from Hexham, and had been befriended by John Middleton Murry and Katherine Mansfield. He was to become very closely associated with Rupert, who nicknamed him affectionately 'Wibson'. His early poetry was in the main romantic and Tennysonian: his second volume, published in 1902, was called *The Queen's Vigil*. Then suddenly he changed direction and began to write about working people and the poor, in *The Stonefolds* (1907) and *Daily Bread* (1910). This new vein was bound to arouse Rupert's interest, and it is clear that he felt at once that Gibson shared his aim of writing more realistically, of breaking through the veil of dreamy, second-hand romanticism that was characteristic of so many of their immediate poetic predecessors, as he himself had in *Channel Passage* and his sonnet about the old age of Menelaus.

Directly after the decision was taken to prepare an anthology of the new poetry, Gibson, Monro and his assistant Arundel del Re (whom Monro had met during a stay in Florence), were invited to luncheon together with another young poet who was new to both Marsh and Rupert, John Drinkwater, a protégé of Monro's, whose *Lyrical and Other Poems* had been published in 1908. Drinkwater maintained afterwards that Lascelles Abercrombie was also present; in any case he very soon became one of this 'inner circle' of young poets. The new venture was eagerly discussed, and the credentials of many of their contemporaries for inclusion closely examined. Walter de la Mare was, in Marsh's view, an obvious candidate, and a few weeks later he took Rupert to meet him over a meal at the Moulin d'Or in Soho. He was fifteen years older than Rupert, six years older than Masefield, and was therefore already forty by the time he was roped in as a contributor to the anthology which it was now decided should be called *Georgian Poetry*. Hardly a new poet; but after the success of his poems for children in *Songs of Childhood* in 1902, he had shown in *The Listeners*, the title poem of the volume he published in 1912, that he was a brilliantly skilful metrical innovator, and on that count alone deserved to be included. Shortly before his death Rupert named him as one of the literary beneficiaries, with Gibson and Abercrombie.

The original idea was that the selections from each poet should consist partly of poems that had recently appeared within the covers of a book, side by side with poems that had not yet been so collected. For Rupert's part in the anthology a small selection was made from his first volume, and to them was added *Grantchester* – which he had at first thought of calling *The Sentimental Exile*. It was agreed that Marsh himself should be editor. Though he had no previous experience of such editorial work, and was not a creative artist himself, he worked swiftly and it seems with complete self-confidence, and the first volume was chosen, printed and ready in the bookshops by December. So began the famous series of *Georgian Poetry*, which was to succeed far beyond Rupert's and Marsh's hopes in making the new poets known to a wide public, and can in fact be said to have dominated English poetic taste until the new revolution inspired by T. S. Eliot changed the scene again less than ten years later.

Rupert was not only a contributor and hidden co-editor to the new venture, but also took charge of publicity. The practical side of his nature was aroused by the challenge, and his letters were full of it. He had slipped off to Berlin again early in November 1912, ostensibly to sort out the copyright in Wedekind's plays, which he wanted to translate; but more probably to put distance again between himself and Ka while he worked hard on the re-writing of his dissertation. 'When I lie awake o' nights,' he wrote to Marsh from the Dudley Wards' home, 'I plan advertisements for "Georgian Poets".' He

made suggestions for getting reviews in Continental papers.
'I'm sure with a little pushing, a good hundred copies could be
sold in Germany and France.' Then there were schemes to
persuade friends and acquaintances to review it in Cambridge
and Oxford papers; and in *The Times* and other London papers.
'I have a hazy vision of incredible *Reklam*, secured by your
potent wire-pulling and ingenious brain.' That was before the
first volume had come out. He appears to have been tireless in
promoting it in the following months, and when he visited
America in the spring he tried to get it published in New York;
but the plan fell through owing to copyright difficulties.

At the same time it is important to realize that Marsh took
a distinctly authoritarian line in his editing, and did not hesitate
to overrule Rupert about inclusions, and choices of poems by
those who were included, in spite of his idolization. 'He's really
got too many rotters in,' Rupert grumbled to Ka in a letter at
the end of September; and then added euphorically, 'But we
all think our fortunes will be made.' And to Marsh, after rather
reluctantly agreeing that the collection should be dedicated to
Robert Bridges (whom he thought 'a fine figure' but Yeats 'worth
a hundred of him'), 'I find myself believing I can make a rival
better selection from the same poets! Of course, I can't set up
to advise you, but I can taunt.'

Marsh's Prefatory Note, written in October, ran as follows:

'This volume is issued in the belief that English poetry is
now once again putting on a new strength and beauty.

Few readers have the leisure or the zeal to investigate
each volume as it appears; and the process of recognition is
often slow. This collection, drawn entirely from the publica-
tions of the past two years, may if it is fortunate help the
lovers of poetry to realize that we are at the beginning of
another "Georgian period" which may take rank in due time
with several great poetic periods of the past.

It has no pretension to cover the field. Every reader will
notice the absence of poets whose work would be a necessary
ornament of any anthology not limited by a definite aim.
Two years ago some of the writers represented had published
nothing; and only a very few of the others were known
except to the eager "watchers of the skies". Those few are

here because within the chosen period their work seemed to have gained some accession of power.'

Whether this could be said to be true of Chesterton (in his late thirties) or Sturge Moore (born 1870) must be open to question. Marsh had also wanted to include Housman, but the author of *The Shropshire Lad* said very sensibly that he did not think he belonged to the 'new era'. On the other side, Marsh had tried to include Ezra Pound (in spite of the fact that he was American), but they failed to agree on the poem to represent him.

The final selection contained six poems by W. H. Davies, five by Rupert himself, five by Walter de la Mare, three each by Wilfred Gibson and James Stephens, two each by Gordon Bottomley, James Elroy Flecker and Harold Monro, and one each by the remainder (though some were long poems or long extracts) – Lascelles Abercrombie, G. K. Chesterton, John Drinkwater, D. H. Lawrence, John Masefield, Sturge Moore, Ronald Ross, Edmund Beale Sargant and R. C. Trevelyan. One wonders which of them Rupert thought 'rotters'. Certainly not those who were already his friends or confederates, de la Mare, Drinkwater, Flecker, Gibson, Masefield, Monro and Abercrombie. And it is extremely unlikely that he was thinking of either Davies or Lawrence; he is known to have admired the latter, at least as a novelist, and Lawrence himself showed immediate sympathy with the idea and was keen to be included. Like Abercrombie who wrote, in an appreciation of Drinkwater, that : 'to any man with brain and spirit active and alert in him, the present is a time wherein the world, and the density of man in the world, are ideas different from anything that has ever been before', Lawrence was soon to claim in similar almost apocalyptic terms that 'we are waking up after a night of oppressive dreams. . . . And now our lungs are full of new air, and our eyes see it is morning.' It is painfully ironic to reflect that the new air was so soon to be filled with phosgene gas.

While Rupert was bombarding him from Berlin with schemes to publicize and extend the sales of the forthcoming book, Marsh was extremely busy himself pulling all the strings he knew in the literary world, sending persuasive letters to editors and critics urging them to do their best to write reviews as favourable as possible, and seeing that it was talked about among his grander social friends. He was a skilful and zealous operator, and the combined efforts of himself and Rupert paid off handsomely.

The story is well known that 'the Prime Minister's car was waiting outside Bumpus's shop in Oxford Street at opening-time on the day of publication'. The reception took even the most sanguine by surprise: *Georgian Poetry 1911–12* went off with a bang, and though many had been sceptical, even some of its well-wishers, it was soon clear that it had awakened a slumbering public interest in poetry. At last something had happened: English poetry had not died amid the languors of the nineties – that seemed to be the reaction of an audience far larger than anyone had imagined possible. Orders poured in to the Poetry Bookshop, and the book had to be reprinted again and again. It went on being reprinted throughout the war (by which time it had been joined by *Georgian Poetry* II and III), and by the end of 1919 it was in its thirteenth thousand and still going strong.

Marsh was a man of some means, and refused to take any fee or royalty for his work as editor. The arrangement between him and Monro was that the Poetry Bookshop kept half the profits, and half was handed over to him to divide up among the contributors, every six months or so. This was a reward for him after his own heart: it meant that he had the best of excuses for keeping constantly in touch with his poets, and for reappearing constantly in their lives as patron and benefactor. One and all were amazed – except perhaps Rupert, who had had a hunch that it was going to happen – and were overflowing with gratitude. De la Mare reckoned that his contribution to the first *Georgian Poetry* had, by 1917, brought him almost as much as his three volumes, *Songs of Childhood, Poems* and *The Listeners* together. And D. H. Lawrence wrote from Italy, in January 1914, 'That *Georgian Poetry* book is a veritable Aladdin's lamp. I little thought my *Snapdragon* would go on blooming and seeding in this prolific fashion.'

7

Critic and Fellow

On his return from his second visit to Berlin towards the end of 1912, Rupert plunged into a tremendous round of parties, luncheons and dinners, and visits to the theatre. He became an *aficionado* of *Hullo Ragtime*, which had just burst on London in all its rowdy and zestful vitality – he saw it ten times. He made several trips to see poet and artist friends, such as Eric Gill and W. H. Davies, in the country. A further trip was to stay with the Cornfords in Cornwall, where he wrote two articles reviewing H. J. C. Grierson's new edition of the poems of John Donne, a landmark in the revival of interest in the work of the great Elizabethan poet. The reviews are especially interesting for the light they throw on his own changing poetic ideals. Admiration for Donne was certainly in the air at Cambridge at the turn of the century, with Lytton Strachey one of the most fervent devotees. Rupert's own interest appears to have been first excited by the enthusiasm of Walter Headlam, at whose feet he had sat in his early days at King's. By 1912 Rupert had come to the conclusion that the supreme period of Elizabethan literature lasted only between 1595 and 1613, a view that he was to expound in his dissertation on Webster, and it was between these two dates that Donne wrote his greatest poetry. 'Donne,' he wrote in the first of these reviews, for the *Nation*, 'applied the same spirit the dramatists applied to the whole world, almost solely to love. He is, for width and depth, incomparably the greatest love-poet in English. . . . Donne's glory is ever increasing. He was the one English love-poet who was not afraid to acknowledge that he was composed of body, soul, and mind; and who faithfully recorded all the pitched battles, alarms, treaties, sieges, and fanfares of that extraordinary triangular warfare.' In his second

review, for *Poetry and Drama* (Monro's successor to the Poetry
Review), he pointed out the specific and unusual nature of that
love poetry: 'The whole composition of the man was made
up of brain, soul and heart in a different proportion from the
ordinary prescription. This does not mean that he felt less keenly
than others; but when passion shook him, and his being ached
for utterance, to relieve the stress, expression came through
the intellect.' He also noted a quality about Donne's poetry
which was to be extremely important for the development of
his own style of poetry, as I have already suggested: his capacity for using unforced colloquialism. 'It has,' he wrote, 'been
the repeated endeavour of half the great English poets to bring
the language of poetry, and the accent and rhythm of poetry,
nearer to those of the intensest moments of common speech.'

Rupert's reviews are, in the majority of cases, pithy, trenchant
and pertinent. They show the constant vigour of a mind
focused exactly upon its object. They are often witty, and
illuminated by imaginative touches; but always serious in
argument and judgement and never fudged by sentimentality
or special pleading. It is easy to conceive that he would have
become one of the leading critics of his day, and not only of
literature but also of the acted play, and even of art, if he had
lived and if he had so wanted. While in Germany he had been
an eager visitor to exhibitions of painting, and came to know
the modern continental masters, from Cézanne and Van Gogh
onwards. The piece he wrote in the *Cambridge Magazine* on
the second Post-Impressionist Exhibition at the Grafton Galleries
shows a wide knowledge of the contemporary artistic scene;
he regretted the absence of Kandinsky from Munich and
Kokoschka from Vienna; praised Matisse as the 'great glory'
of the exhibition (though he expressed disappointment at the
lack of colour in Picasso's work). He was cautious about the
work exhibited by his friend Duncan Grant, complaining that
'his genius is an elusive and faithless sprite'. In general he found
that the English contribution hardly stood up to the best from
the Continent.

At the same time he was delivering lectures and working on
new poems, and seemed, with his anxieties about Ka partly
allayed by her departure for abroad, to have recovered a great
deal of his astonishing energy, though scarcely his former
buoyancy: the old Rupert had gone for ever. The disconcerting

change in his attitude to the world since his break with Bloomsbury was unpleasantly underlined by his growing anti-Semitism
and anti-Feminism. He had been thrilled by his early visits to
the Russian Ballet, but now announced, in a lecture at Cambridge, that it was 'handicapped by the extremely tawdry and
inharmonious scenery and dresses of a Russian Jew called
Bakst'. In Munich, and afterwards for a long while, he almost
hero-worshipped Ibsen as *the* modern dramatist; now, because
Ibsen was a protagonist of Feminism, he had become that 'great
and dirty playwright Ibsen', and Strindberg had become his
idol because Feminism 'disgusted' him.

In Berlin he had worked hard on the polishing of his dissertation, making certain important changes as a result of his meetings and discussions there with the critic-philosopher T. E.
Hulme. At the end of the year he put the final touches to it,
and sent it in to his judges at King's. Early in February he heard
that he had succeeded and was to be elected a Fellow.

In the version published after his death, in 1916, the dissertation, which was called *John Webster and the Elizabethan
Drama*, consists of five chapters with a short preface, totalling
something between 30,000 and 35,000 words. The dissertation
proper is followed by ten appendices, considerably longer in
all than the main text, almost entirely devoted to an examination of the claims of the disputed plays to Webster's authorship.

It starts with three chapters which are brief studies of the
Elizabethan theatre as a whole, its origins, the way it developed,
its characteristics and changing nature as the original impulse
decayed and was altered by succeeding fashions of the times
and the different temperaments of new poets. This early part
is full of rather sweeping, slapdash generalizations, in which
one feels that the author was mischievously trailing his coat
in the face of the established scholars – and also making himself rather silly by a prime desire to shock. It betrays the strong
influence of G. E. Moore's philosophy and way of argument, as
the following quotation shows: 'One is reduced to saying that
a good play means a play that would be likely to stir good states
of mind in an intelligent man of the same nation, class and
century as the author. It follows that a good Elizabethan play
is a play that would have been good in Elizabethan times; and
not a play that is good to us, with our different ideas. The two
categories coincide to a great extent. But their differences are

important.' The author also indulges in a reckless swipe at 'history' plays, holding them up to scorn as 'a transient, dreary, childish kind' (one must suppose that this dismissal includes *Henry IV* Parts 1 and 2), and goes on to maintain that, with the exception of *A Midsummer Night's Dream*, Shakespeare's romantic comedies have nothing but an 'undistinguished prettiness' and a 'pink Magic' that Shakespeare has thrown over them. The same prettiness, only sloppier, Rupert claims, ruins the plays of Beaumont and Fletcher, which are simply decadent. Tragedy is all; and the supreme period only lasts between 1600 and 1610.

If Rupert had kept up this aggressive tone throughout the dissertation, it seems unlikely that he would have got his Fellowship. When, however, he gets down to John Webster himself in his last two chapters, he reveals himself as a serious, highly intelligent scholar, sensitive as only a poet can be to the nuances of diction and style, the characteristic imagery and imaginative mood that distinguishes the dramatist he is studying. One cannot help feeling that his own emotional upheaval in 1912 deepened his sympathetic response to Webster's obsession with jealousy, ruin and the darkness of fate. He also takes up John Addington Symonds's idea that Webster used a notebook to jot down passages and phrases that had impressed him in his reading, and argues persuasively that the chief sources must have been Sidney's *Arcadia*, Montaigne and Donne.

'The chief value [he writes] of working through a notebook, from a literary point of view, is this. A man tends to collect quotations, phrases, and ideas, that particularly appeal to and fit in with his own personality. If that personality is a strong one, and the point of his work is the pungency with which it is imbued with this strong taste, the not too injudicious agglutination of these external fragments will vastly enrich and heighten the total effect. And this is, on the whole, what happens with Webster. The heaping-up of images and phrases helps to confuse and impress the hearer, and gives body to a taste that might otherwise have been too thin to carry. Webster, in fine, belongs to the caddisworm school of writers, who do not become their complete selves until they are encrusted with a thousand orts and chips and fragments from the world around.'

For Rupert, the indubitably great plays are *The White Devil* and *The Duchess of Malfi*. He is prepared to accept *The Devil's Law-Case* as Webster's, though considering it much inferior to the two masterpieces, and, with considerable reservations, *A Cure for Cuckolds*. He deals with these two plays in more detail in the Appendices, where he also deals with the other plays which have, at one time or another, been attributed to Webster. All these studies show close knowledge of previous scholarship, and provide a careful and sensitive examination of the language, situations, and poetic personalities that are revealed in the doubtful plays. Particularly interesting is the close analysis with which he demonstrates his conclusion that Thomas Heywood was the author mainly responsible for *Appius and Virginia*; though one must add that his arguments are not generally accepted by later scholars.

All in all, the dissertation is an impressive achievement, and fully merits the praise F. L. Lucas accorded it in his own edition of Webster in 1927:

'On the literary side Webster's youngest critic – Rupert Brooke will always remain that – is still, I think, his best. *John Webster and the Elizabethan Drama* is indeed a very youthful book: that is why it is so good. Its author had not time to amass the mountainous erudition which goes with much modern study of the Elizabethans: but another quality, rare in commentators and even more essential here, he did possess – he was alive to the finger-tips. And accordingly he not only did his share in clearing up the facts of Webster's work: he seems to me to have done more than anyone else to place that work, without exaggerating its faults or ignoring them, in its just position among the lasting possessions of English literature. From the exclamations of Lamb and the roarings of Swinburne on the one hand, as from the outcries of Kingsley and Archer and Shaw on the other, it is to him that one learns to come back in search of sanity.'

8

The Living Root

Three days after Rupert received the news of his Fellowship
Marsh gave a dinner party in his rooms which was in effect a
celebration of his protégé's success. This was, I think one may
say, a decisive event in his life because not only was Yeats
there, but it was the first occasion on which he met some of
Marsh's grand friends, who were destined to take him ever
further away from the Bloomsbury circle of the past. Among
the guests were Violet Asquith, the daughter of the Prime
Minister, Lady Cynthia Asquith, and the wife of the man Marsh
was now working for as Secretary at the Admiralty, 'Clemmie' –
Mrs Winston Churchill. Violet Asquith was to become a close
friend, to whom he addressed many of his most revealing and
lively letters from now on. She appeared again at another
dinner, or rather supper party at Marsh's chambers in the early
spring, together with the already famous society beauty, Lady
Diana Manners. And on 15 April a birthday dinner was given
at No. 10 Downing Street for Violet, at which the guests – 'a
most extraordinary conglomeration,' Rupert told his mother –
included literary lions such as Bernard Shaw, James Barrie and
John Masefield, together with the prominent Liberal politicians
of the day, Lord Haldane and Augustine Birrell. Soon after, on
9 May, Marsh left for an official tour of the Mediterranean in
the Admiralty yacht *Enchantress*, with Winston Churchill and
the Asquiths.

Rupert would hardly have been human if, at the age of
twenty-six, he had not been dazzled and deeply flattered by
the attentions of these Top People, to whom his adoring Eddie
Marsh had sung his praises so assiduously, and no doubt continued to sing them on the *Enchantress* cruise. If his head was
turned, it was to a large extent because they provided such a

brilliant and reassuring substitute for his old friends, who had now turned into demons in his mind; that they had power and influence may well have obscured the fact that, highly intelligent though they were, they had neither the intellectual nor the creative eminence of Bloomsbury.

At the same time another extremely important element had entered his life. To Marsh's supper party in early December the young actress Cathleen Nesbitt had been invited, perhaps because Rupert, a month or two before, had seen her playing in *The Winter's Tale*, which had been put on by Granville-Barker at the Savoy, and had been entranced by her performance and her personality.* She was sixteen months younger than Rupert (not three years, as Hassall asserts), but looked even younger. With dark hair, delicate features and a look of sensitive innocence, she was Perdita to perfection: to Rupert she appears to have represented a creature totally unspoilt and unspotted by the 'uncleanness' which obsessed his mind in connection with his earlier friendships and emotional involvements. She had been reading *Georgian Poetry*, she tells us in her autobiography, and mentioned to the blushing Rupert that she had particularly admired a poem called *Heaven* by a young man called Rupert Brooke. This perhaps clinched it, but it seems that he had already fallen for her. (In fact the poem was not *Heaven*, but *The Fish*, the original version.) In the following weeks he saw as much as possible of her: a diffident but increasingly devoted suitor. In his edition of Rupert's letters, Sir Geoffrey Keynes writes: 'In her company his more normal feelings revived, and she was from thenceforwards to play the main part in his emotional life.' He was still profoundly troubled by his relationship with Ka, and at the back of his mind guilty, too, about the way he had behaved to Noel Olivier. Cathleen Nesbitt was, in a sense, a life-line out of the quicksands, a hope for his future. In some ways he was surprisingly shy in his approach to her, as his letter to Marsh at the end of January shows:

'It *had* just occurred to me, that, as Mrs. Ervine has to go on from us to the theatre, & we shall probably pick her

* There is some confusion in Hassall's account of the meeting. At the time of the supper party Miss Nesbitt was no longer playing in *The Winter's Tale* but in *The Eldest Son*.

up there afterwards, and as they know her, & as it's so ridiculously convenient, we might include in the party, on one or other occasion, quite incidentally – oh dear me! – Cathleen. But no doubt it's quite impossible – I suppose she dines with Millionaires every night – I can see a thousand insuperable difficulties – it was scarcely worth while mentioning it. . . .'

Nevertheless by the beginning of March he had become sufficiently involved with her to write to her a letter, the first surviving letter of all he was to write to her which could be described as a deeply committed love letter, if it were not that it gives a slight suggestion of artifice, in the midst of the hyperbolic phrases (and the expletives), almost the courtly Knight to his Lady :

'I adore you.
  I was in a stupor all yesterday; partly because of my tiredness, and partly because of your face.
  I'm gradually getting normal again.
  Why do you look like that? Have you any idea what you look like? I didn't know that human beings could look like that. It's as far beyond beauty as beauty is beyond ugliness.
  I'd say you were beautiful if the word weren't a million times too feeble.
  Hell!
  But it's very amazing.
  It makes me nearly imbecile when I'm talking to you – I apologize for my imbecility : it's your fault. You shouldn't look like that.
  It really makes life very much worth while. My God!
  I adore you.'

He poured out more letters to her in the same strain :

'I am infinitely thankful that you exist.
  Your eyes are well set in, and very lovely. They change a great deal, from the beauty of softness to the beauty of light; so that I don't even know what colour they are (I do in a way) : but they're always lovely.
  It was well thought of that your nose should have that ripple in the middle. If you had had a straight individual

nose, you might merely have been a goddess. You're something far more wonderful and beautiful.

The lines of your cheek and jaw – the Greeks may have *dreamt* of that, I think. They tried to get something of that effect in stone, once or twice – poor bunglers!'

Cathleen does not appear to have taken them altogether seriously, and teased him about them. Once again he was in bed with a fever (his temperature seemed to shoot up with his hyperboles), and he was stung:

'You say that I get drunk on my own words. It is a thing no lady should say to a gentleman. I daresay Irish girls are very badly brought up. I had a good mind to reply with a lot of dirty insults in German. I'll have you know that I am entirely, deplorably, cynically sober. . . . I refuse to be bullied by your knowledge of mankind. I have written no sonnets to you, yet (and when I *do*, they'll be a damn sight better than what you quote). I merely state the fact that you are incomparably beautiful. It would be absurd to be intoxicated by phrases. . . .'

In spite of these rather tart exchanges, the real feeling between them was growing. He saw her whenever he could get her away from the theatre. As often as possible, at week-ends, he would take her out of London and tramp the countryside with her, sometimes staying the night at an hotel or inn, where after supper he would read Donne and Shakespeare to her. Miss Nesbitt recalls that they always had separate rooms, and never became actual lovers. He would come into her room and talk and talk to her, and put his head sometimes on her bed and go to sleep; but always returned to his own room for the night; a situation that was less strange then than it seems today. Ka was still away in Eastern Europe, and so her propinquity could not come between them. He felt an ever-increasing need for Cathleen; and when there was talk of her going on a tour to America with a theatrical company, he wrote her an immensely long letter, giving as many reasons as he could think of for her not to go, above all for her not to leave him:

'If you could see sometimes in my mind, you'd understand how desperately frightened and miserable I become at the thought of you going away. Dear love, I've been through

evil places and I cling all the more graspingly to the peace
and comfort I find more and more in loving you and being
with you. It grows as I see love in you for me grow. Love
in me grows slowly, and differently from the old ways – I
thought the root was gone. But it's still there. It's the one
thing I've got, to love you, and feel love growing, and the
strength and peace growing, and to learn to worship you, and
to want to protect you, to desire both to possess every atom
of your body and soul, and yet to lose myself in your kindliness, like a child. It must be that, in the end, it wouldn't do,
and we'd find that I didn't love you enough, or you me. But
there's the hope and the great chance. We're so far towards
it. The more I know you, the more I love. And the more I
know and love, the more I find you have to give me, and
I to give you. How can I let this growing glory and hope be
broken, and let myself go adrift again? . . . I want to love and
to work. I don't want to be washed about on these doubtful
currents and black waves or drift into some dingy corner of
the tide.'

In spite of this impassioned appeal to Cathleen, the curious,
and perhaps paradoxical, fact remains that within a month
of writing he had decided to go on a long tour of America
himself. The friends, above all Frances Cornford, who had
witnessed his utter confusion and distress in the aftermath of
his breakdown the year before had urged him for a long time
to go. He hesitated, and changed his mind again and again.
His mother had originally been very much against it; but she
had finally seen that she could only increase his determination
by opposing it, and yielded, sadly.

It was not until after Rupert's death that Cathleen met his
mother. She was struck at once by her inflexible character and
the 'strong stubborn puritanism' which she had passed on to
her son, and which he struggled to free himself from, in the
end so unavailingly. She had reservations about meeting 'the
actress' who seemed to have been so important in the last phase
of Rupert's life; but when they eventually did meet they at
once became good friends, and she was persuaded to be god-
mother to Cathleen's first son after her marriage to Cecil
Ramage. Cathleen herself never ceased to regret that she had
not had a son by Rupert.

9

A Small Boy and Sixpence

On 22 May 1913 Rupert left on his travels to America and further west. On his last evening he said goodbye to a group of his friends, who included Wilfred Gibson, Geoffrey Keynes and Middleton Murry, at a party in a dive off Regent Street. It was noticeable that James Strachey was not present and had not been invited, though there is some reason to believe that Rupert was at the last distressed that his very old and loyal, but rejected, friend was not with them. He did in fact write to him from his travels, though one detects a certain lack of the old spontaneity in the letters. Marsh was away in the Mediterranean, dancing attendance on Winston Churchill. Two faithful friends, St John Lucas and Denis Browne, saw him off at Euston, en route for Liverpool and the *Cedric*. By this time Denis Browne, who had been Rupert's junior at Cambridge by one year, had begun a friendship with Marsh which was to grow steadily more intimate and affectionate. He became, in fact, closer to Marsh among his young friends than anyone except Rupert, and consoled Marsh during Rupert's long absences.

There was no one on the quayside at Liverpool for a last farewell. He suddenly felt rather lonely. He gave sixpence to a small boy called William to wave to him as the ship set off on its voyage. William obliged, and waved and shouted messages until he could no longer be seen or heard. 'The last object I looked at was a small dot waving a white handkerchief (or nearly white) faithfully.'

Loneliness came back over him like a wave. Then suddenly, to his joy, he discovered that Cathleen had not forgotten.

'I arrived solitary on the boat [he wrote to her]. After it had started I asked at the office – more to show that I existed than in the dimmest hope of getting anything – were there

any letters for Rupert Brooke. And out, astonishingly, came
a letter and a telegram; and both from divine *you*. And the
letter you'd been writing all those last good days, secretly!
Was there ever so nice a person? The *fact* you'd written it
upset me more than I can say. And then the letter itself!
I sat on my bed and laughed and cried over it. And two hours
later I went past again, and there was, stuck up, a list called
"Unclaimed Mail". (I thought it sounded as if a lot of knights
who had promised to equip themselves for the quest of the
Holy Grail, had missed the train, or married a wife, or over
slept, or something) – and at the top of the list "Mr. Rupert
Brooke". "Good God!" I thought, "there is somebody else
who has remembered my existence!" But there wasn't!
There was only that absurd Cathleen again, sending a silver
boot, of all mad things in the world! You can't think how
it cheered me up, this string of communication with you. It
felt as if your love was so strong it reached with me all the
way. It's queer. I do feel as if [there] was a lovely and present
guardianship all the time. My darling, you give me so much
more than I deserve. But it does make me feel so quiet and
secure.'

Just before he left, Naomi Royde Smith, still literary editor
of the *Westminster Gazette*, to which he had contributed so
often over so many years, persuaded the editor-in-chief, J. A.
Spender, to commission a series of articles from him about his
travels. This made a vital difference to his finances for the trip,
as his own funds were low. Indeed it is doubtful whether he
could have travelled anything like as far or as long as he did
if it had not been for this providential assignment.

The thirteen articles he wrote duly appeared in the *Westminster*, and were republished after his death, in 1916, with
two other articles he sent to the *New Statesman*. The book contained a long introductory effusion, of an embarrassingly hero-
worshipping character, by Henry James: one of the last – and
most lamentable – pieces the Master produced before his death
in the same year.

There was not much to chronicle on the crossing, and it was
not mentioned in the articles. But he did encounter his first
American Big Business Man, as he wrote to Marsh:

'I found sitting next to me at table a little man of fifty with

Ottawa 1913:
Rupert with
Duncan Campbell Scott

Taata Mata, Tahiti 1914

Cathleen Nesbitt as Jessica in *The Merchant of Venice* (*Radio Times Hulton Picture Library*)

Rupert with members
of the Hood Battalion
of the Royal Naval
Division

Rupert's first grave on
the island of Skyros,
1915

The memorial plaque to Rupert Brooke in Rugby School Chapel

a cold light-blue eye, with a pleasant turn of American humour. He appeared to be interested in theatres, so I took him into the smoking-room and delivered a lecture on Modern Drama in England, America and Germany, on Theatre-managing, on Commercialism in the Drama, and many other such topics. I got on to *The Great Adventure*: which he thought the best entertainment in London. I patted him on the head. "Yep," he said, "I've just sent a marconi-*gram* to buy that play for America." I said, "Oh, have you a theatre in America?" He said, "In New York I own the Grand Opera House, the Metropolitan Theatre, the Gaiety, and seven more. I have some in every big town in the States. I'm coming back with a new Lehar, a Bernstein, two German comedies. . . ." I forget the rest. He turns out to be Klaw, of Klaw and Erlanger. I felt a little like Dominic [Spring-Rice], when he saw a lonely girl at a fancy-dress dance the other day, and took her out to dance, and it was Karsavina.'

Rupert's itinerary took him from New York to Boston, and then on to Canada – Montreal, Ottawa, Quebec and the Saguenay river, Ontario, Niagara Falls and Winnipeg. From there he made an expedition into the wilds of the north, then crossed the Rockies to Vancouver. A new acquaintance he had made in New York, Russell Loines, a lawyer and a friend of Goldie Lowes Dickinson, gave him an introduction to Professor Chauncey Wells of the University of California, and from the west coast of Canada he set off for San Francisco. Both Loines and Wells took a strong liking to him, and Loines in particular proved a staunch and valuable friend, in the event lending him enough money to carry out the plan he had long had at the back of his mind, which was to visit the South Seas. He left California on 7 October, having completed the series of articles he had signed up to write for Spender.

The *Westminster* articles reveal a new side to Rupert's talents, as an accomplished travel-writer. They are written with a restrained and graceful skill; the general tone is sophisticated and urbane, with a continual undertone of irony and humour. His descriptions of people he met, and above all places he visited, are witty and imaginative; and some of the bravura pieces, for instance the pictures of Niagara Falls and of Lake Louise, are fresh and poetic and exact. They undoubtedly strengthen the view of some of his contemporaries that his eventual literary career could have been even more as a prose writer than as a poet.

Landing in New York, his first impressions of America were overwhelming. He was struck above all by the way men dressed and walked along the streets.

'The American by race [he wrote in his second article] walks better than us; more freely, with a taking swing, and almost with grace. How much of this is due to living in a democracy, and how much to wearing no braces, it is very difficult to determine. But certainly it is the land of belts, and therefore of more loosely moving bodies. This, and the padded shoulder of the coats, and the loosely cut trousers, make a figure more presentable, at a distance, than most urban civilizations turn out. Also, Americans take off their coats, which is sensible; and they can do it the more beautifully because they are belted, and not braced. They take their coats off anywhere and anywhen, and somehow it strikes the visitor as the most symbolic thing about them. They have not yet thought of discarding collars; but they are unashamedly shirt-sleeved. Any sculptor, seeking to figure their Republic in stone, must carve, in future, a young man in shirtsleeves, open-faced, and rather vulgar, straw hat on the back of his head, his trousers full and sloppy, his coat over his arm. The motto written beneath will be, of course, "This is some country".'

The other aspect of America that struck him at once was the commercialism, the supremacy of Business, and therefore of advertising. 'Business,' he wrote, 'has developed insensibly into a Religion, in more than the light, metaphorical sense of the word. It has its ritual and theology, its high places and its jargon, as well as its priests and martyrs. America has a childlike faith in advertising. They advertise here, there, everywhere, and in all ways. Nothing is untouched.' He then goes on to describe, deadpan fashion with tongue in cheek, and with a sly parody of Walter Pater in passing, some of the more extraordinary manifestations of the advertising craze, keeping up his theme of its pseudo-religious inspiration:

'Cities, like cats, will reveal themselves at night. There comes an hour of evening when lower Broadway, the business end of town, is deserted. And if, having felt yourself immersed in men and the frenzy of cities all day, you stand out in the street in this sudden hush, you will hear, like a strange questioning voice from another world, the melancholy boom of a foghorn, and realize that not half a mile away are the waters of the sea, and some great liner making its slow way out to the Atlantic. After that, the lights come out up-town, and the New York of theatres and vaudevilles and restaurants begins to roar and flare. The merciless lights throw a mask of unradiant glare on the human beings in the streets, making each face hard, set, wolfish, terribly blue. . . . Cars shriek down the street; the Elevated train clangs and curves perilously overhead; newsboys wail the baseball news; wits cry their obscure challenges to one another, "I should worry!" or "She's some daisy!" or "Goodnight, Nurse!" In houses off the streets around children are being born, lovers are kissing, people are dying. Above, in the midst of the coruscating divinities, sits one older and greater than any. Most colossal of all, it flashes momently out, a woman's head, all flame against the darkness. It is beautiful, passionless, in its simplicity and conventional representation queerly like an archaic Greek or early Egyptian figure. Queen of the night behind, and of the gods around, and of the city below – here, if at all, you think, may one find the answer to the riddle. Her ostensible message, burning in the firmament beside her, is that we should buy pepsin chewing-gum. But there is more, not to be given in words, ineffable. Suddenly, when she has surveyed mankind, she closes her left eye. Three times she winks, and then vanishes. No ordinary winks these, but portentous, terrifyingly steady, obliterating a great tract of the sky. Hour by hour she does this, night by night, year by year. That enigmatic obscuration of light, that answer that is no answer, is, perhaps the first thing in this world that a child born near here will see, and the last thing a dying man will have to take for a message to the curious dead. She is immortal. Men have worshipped her as Isis and as Ashtaroth, as Venus, as Cybele, Mother of the Gods, and as Mary. There is a statue of her by the steps of the British Museum. Here, above the fantastic civilization she observes, she has no name.

She is older than the skyscrapers amongst which she sits; and one, certainly, of her eyelids is a trifle weary. And the only answer to our cries, the only comment upon our cities, is that divine stare, the wink, once, twice, thrice. And then darkness.'

After an expedition by canoe seventy miles up the Delaware River with Russell Loines, the goal of which was a lonely farmhouse where an artist friend of Loines lived, he left New York for Boston and Harvard. Boston he found 'homely after New York. The Boston crowd is curiously English. They have nice eighteenth century houses there, and ivy grows on the buildings.' He realized at once that the great age of Boston had passed. 'It used to lead America in Literature, Thought, Art, everything. The years have passed. It is remarkable how nearly now Boston is to New York what Munich is to Berlin. Boston and Munich were the leaders forty years ago. They can't quite make out that they aren't now. It is too incredible that Art should leave her goose-feather bed and away to the wraggle-taggle business men. And certainly, if Berlin and New York are more "live", Boston and Munich are more themselves, less feverishly imitations of Paris. But the undisputed palm is there no more; and its absence is felt.'

He did not stay long in the city, but went across the river to Cambridge and Harvard. He was taken at once by the charm of the University. 'Harvard is a spirit, a way of looking at things, austerely refined, gently moral, kindly. The perception of it grows on the foreigner. Its charm is so deliciously old in this land, so deliciously young compared with the lovely frowst of Oxford and Cambridge. You see it in temperament, the charm of simplicity and good-heartedness and culture; in the Harvard undergraduate, who is a boy, while his English contemporary is either a young man or a schoolboy, less pleasant stages; and in the old Bostonian who heard, and still hears, the lectures of Dickens and Thackeray.' Time seemed to have stopped for these old Bostonians, and their glance was backward, their whole awareness was of the past; but without nostalgia – how could one be nostalgic for what one believed to be still existing? – rather with satisfaction and pride: 'They are the flower of a civilization, its ripest critics, and final judges. Carlyle and Emerson are their greatest living heroes. One of them bent the kindliness and alert interest of his eighty years

Rupert Brooke (right)
with his brother Alfred
in 1900

Rupert's mother,
'the Ranee'

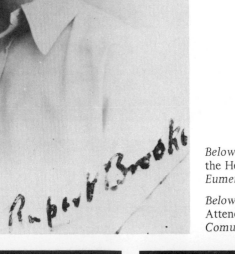

Rugby 1906: Rupert as
schoolboy cricketer

Below left: Rupert as
the Herald in the
Eumenides

Below: Rupert as the
Attendant Spirit in
Comus (1908)

Noel Olivier, camping
out in 1909

Brynhild Olivier and Justin
Brooke at Clifford's Bridge,
1909

Rupert Brooke in the
New Forest, 1909

The Old Vicarage,
Grantchester

Rupert on the Cam, with
Dudley Ward behind

The announcement that was
sent to the parents of the
boys at School House in
January 1910

SCHOOL HOUSE,
RUGBY.

I am deeply grieved to inform you that your son's
House Master, MR. W. P. BROOKE, died yesterday
evening after a short illness.

The funeral is fixed for Thursday afternoon, the first
part of the Service will be held in the School Chapel at 2.

In accordance with the wish of Mrs. Brooke the boys
will return with the rest of the School on the evening of
that day.

For the ensuing Term I am placing the House in the
charge of Mr. Rupert Brooke, B.A., of King's College,
Cambridge.

The new House Master, of whom you shall be informed
a little later, will enter upon his duties in May next.

Rugby,   A. A. DAVID.
25th January, 1910.

Rupert at work, outside
the Old Vicarage

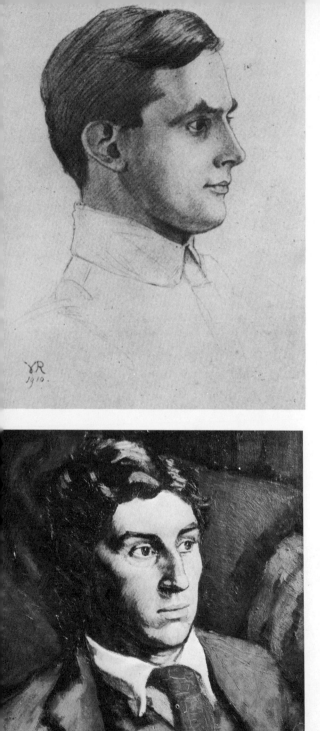

Edward Marsh in 1910:
a drawing by Violet,
Duchess of Rutland

Jacques Raverat, painted
by Gwen Darwin

Ka Cox in 1912

Ka Cox in 1911: a
drawing by Henry Lamb

Sonnet

Oh! Death will find me, long before I tire
  Of watching you; and swing me suddenly
Into the shade and loneliness and mire
  Of the last land! There, waiting patiently,

One day, I think, I'll feel a cool wind blowing,
  See a slow light across the Stygian tide,
And hear the Dead about me stir, unknowing,
  And tremble. And _I_ shall know that you have died,

And watch you, a broad-browed and smiling dream,
  Pass, light as ever, through the lightless host,
Quietly ponder, start, and sway, and gleam —
  Most individual and bewildering ghost! —

And turn, and toss your brown delightful head
Amusedly, among the ancient Dead.

                                    Rupert Brooke

March 24 1912

A poem written by Rupert Brooke in Edward Marsh's
Commonplace Book

upon me. "So you come from Rugby," he said. "Tell me, do you know that curious creature, Matthew Arnold?" I couldn't bring myself to tell him that even in Rugby, we had forgiven that brilliant youth his iconoclastic tendencies some time since, and that, as a matter of fact, he had died when I was eight months old.'

The strangest, most completely American phenomenon he witnessed, stranger even than the baseball game he attended, which he compared to glorified rounders, was the parade during the Harvard Commencement of alumni who had assembled to take their places before the game:

'There entered to us, across the field, a troop of several hundred men, all dressed in striped shirts of the same hue and pattern, and headed by a vast banner which informed the world that they were the graduates of 1910, celebrating their triennial. In a military formation they moved across the plain towards us, led by a band, ceaselessly vociferating, and raising their straw hats in unison to mark the time. Then followed the class of 1907, attired as sailors; 1903, the decennial class, with some samples of their male children marching with them, and a banner inscribed "515 Others. No race suicide"; 1898, carefully arranged in an H-shaped formation, dancing along to their music with a slow polka-step, each with his hands on the shoulders of the man in front, and at the head of all their leader, dancing backwards in perfect time, marshalling them; 1888, middle-aged men, again with some children, and a Highland regiment playing the bagpipes.'

Rupert's impressions of the United States are so fresh and alive that one is inclined to regret that he didn't explore further in New England, though on his return from the South Seas he visited Washington and Chicago, when his mind was full of island impressions; but he seemed determined to get away to Canada, perhaps longing for wider open spaces that might provide balm for his still-troubled spirit. In the Dominion he noted at once the distinct Englishness, in many small and often undefinable ways, of the Anglo-Saxon cities, and the sharp difference between them and the French cities, a difference equally sharp where the two races lived side by side as in Montreal: 'Inter-marriage is very rare. They do not meet socially; only on business, and that not very often. In the same city these two communities dwell side by side, with different traditions, different languages, different ideals, without sympathy or comprehension.' At the same time he came to the conclusion that though 'the French and British in Canada seem to have behaved with quite extraordinary generosity and kindliness towards one another', the deeper cultural division produced 'that kind of ill-health which afflicts men who are cases of "double personality" – debility and spiritual paralysis.' It disturbed him; he saw no easy solution.

As he travelled further into the country, he became more and more aware of two dominant characteristics, or flaws. The first was a commercialism, a get-rich-quick mentality as narrowing as in the States, in particular an obsession with land values as the cities grew and encroached further upon virgin territory. This he found especially exaggerated in the West:

> 'I travelled from Edmonton to Calgary in the company of a citizen of Edmonton and a citizen of Calgary. Hour after hour they disputed. Land in Calgary had risen from five dollars to three hundred. Edmonton had grown from thirty persons to forty thousand in twenty years; but Calgary from twenty to thirty thousand in twelve. . . . "Where" – as a respite – "did I come from?" I had to tell them, not without shame, that my own town of Grantchester, having numbered three hundred at the time of Julius Caesar's landing, had risen rapidly to nearly four by Domesday Book, but was now declined to three-fifty. They seemed perplexed and angry.'

His gloomy conclusion was that the 'old pioneers of the West', the 'finest people in Canada', were dying out or powerless before the onset of a new generation with very different values.

> 'The tragedy of the West is that these men have passed, and what they lived and died to secure for their race is now the foundation for a gigantic national gambling of a most unprofitable and disastrous kind. Hordes of people – who mostly seem to come from the great neighbouring Commonwealth, and are inspired with the national hunger for getting rich quickly without deserving it – prey on the community by their dealings in what is humorously called "Real Estate".

For them our fathers died. What a sowing, and what a harvest! And where good men worked or perished is now a row of little shops, all devoted to the sale of town-lots in some distant spot that must infallibly become a great city in the next two years, and in the doorway of each lounges a thin-chested, much spitting youth, with a flabby face, shifty eyes, and an inhuman mouth, who invites you continually, with the most raucous of American accents, to "step inside and ex-amine our Praposition".'

The other dominant characteristic that struck Rupert, as a poet especially and as a lover of his ancient home country of England, was the contrast between the magnificent beauty of the Canadian natural scene and its spiritual emptiness. He realized, it seems to his dismay, what other pioneers of virgin landscape had discovered before him, that breath-taking as the splendour of mountains, forests, lakes and rivers may be, it may fail to have any profounder meaning to the heart and imagination without human association. In his first, sensitive impression of the wild country beyond Winnipeg this realization is already apparent, though delight is still uppermost:

'It is that feeling of fresh loneliness that impresses itself before any detail of the wild. The soul – or the personality – seems to have indefinite room to expand. There is no one else within reach, there never has been anyone; no one else is *thinking* of the lakes and hills you see before you. They have no tradition, no names even; they are only pools of water and lumps of earth, some day, perhaps, to be clothed with loves and memories and the comings and goings of men, but now dumbly awaiting their Wordsworth or their Acropolis to give them individuality, and a soul. In such country as this there is a rarefied clean sweetness. The air is unbreathed, and the earth untrodden. All things share this childlike loveliness, the grey whispering reeds, the pure blue of the sky, the birches and thin fir-trees that make up these forests, even the brisk touch of the clear water as you dive.'

Later, however, among the Rockies, the sense of disappointment and absence had gained on him, and he was defining more precisely:

'It is an empty land. To love the country here – mountains
are worshipped, not loved – is like embracing a wraith. A
European can find nothing to satisfy the hunger of his heart.
The air is too thin to breathe. He requires haunted woods,
and the friendly presence of ghosts. . . . The maple and the
birch conceal no dryads, and Pan has never been heard
amongst these reed-beds. Look as long as you like upon a
cataract of the New World, you shall not see a white arm
in the foam. A godless place. And the dead do not return.
That is why there is nothing lurking in the heart of the
shadows, and no human mystery in the colours, and neither
the same joy nor the kind of peace in dawn and sunset that
older lands know. It is, indeed, a new world. How far away
seem those grassy, moonlit places in England that have been
Roman camps or roads, where there is always serenity, and
the spirit of a purpose at rest, and the sunlight flashes upon
more than flint! Here one is perpetually a first-comer. The
land is virginal, the wind cleaner than elsewhere, and every
lake new-born, and each day is the first day. The flowers are
less conscious than English flowers, the breezes have nothing
to remember, and everything to promise. There walk, as yet,
no ghosts of lovers in Canadian lanes. This is the essence of
the grey freshness and brisk melancholy of this land. And
for all the charm of those qualities it is also the secret of a
European's discontent. For it is possible, at a pinch, to do
without gods. But one misses the dead.'

Rupert's response to the atmosphere of place and his powers
of evocation were remarkable all through his travels. He reacted
almost with violence to the Saguenay river, a tributary which
comes into the St Lawrence about one hundred and thirty miles
from Quebec, during a trip he had been recommended to take
very soon after his arrival in that city. The St Lawrence he
thought 'the most glorious river in the world'; his impression
of the Saguenay, from the moment his boat in 'almost full
night' entered it, could not have been more different. It was
as if it imaged something in himself, from which he had been
trying to escape:

'Darkness hid all detail, and we were only aware of vast
cliffs, sometimes dense with trees, sometimes bare faces of
sullen rock. They shut us in, oppressively, but without heat.

There are no banks to this river, for the most part; only these walls, rising sheer from the water to the height of two thousand feet, going down sheer beneath it, or rather by the side of it, to many times that depth. The water was of some colour blacker than black. Even by daylight it is inky and sinister. It flows without foam or ripple. No white showed in the wake of the boat. The ominous shores were without sign of life, save for a rare light every few miles, to mark some bend in the chasm. Once a canoe with two Indians shot out of the shadows, passed under our stern, and vanished silently down stream. We all became hushed and apprehensive. The night was gigantic and terrible. There were a few stars, but the flood slid along too swiftly to reflect them. The whole scene seemed some Stygian imagination of Dante. As we drew further and further into that lightless land, little twists and curls of vapour wriggled over the black river-surface. Our homeless, irrelevant, tiny steamer seemed to hang between two abysms. One became suddenly aware of the miles of dark water beneath. I found that under a prolonged gaze the face of the river began to writhe and eddy, as if from some horrible suppressed emotion. It seemed likely that something might appear. I reflected that if the river failed us, all hope was gone; and that anyhow this region was the abode of devils. I went to bed.'

Many travellers have described Niagara Falls; it is hardly possible to do so now without falling into repetition and cliché. Nevertheless nearly seven decades ago the impression it made on Rupert evoked one of his subtlest virtuoso pieces of nature painting, and for that reason is worth quoting. 'Niagara means nothing,' he insists at the beginning. 'It is merely a great deal of water falling over some cliffs. But it is very remarkably that.' He was appalled at first by its commercial exploitation as a unique beauty spot. 'Niagara is the central home and breeding place for all the touts of earth ... who have no apparent object in the world, but just purely, simply, merely, incessantly, indefatigably – to tout.' The sight of the Falls immediately expunged from the mind this bedlam of salesmanship. 'He who sees them instantly forgets humanity,' he recorded. He began by describing the Canadian side of the island which divides them:

'Half a mile or so above the Falls, on either side, the water of the great stream begins to run more swiftly and in confusion. It descends with ever-growing speed. It begins chattering and leaping, breaking into a thousand ripples, throwing up joyful fingers of spray. Sometimes it is divided by islands and rocks, sometimes the eye can see nothing but a waste of laughing, springing, foamy waves, turning, crossing, even seeming to stand for an instant erect, but always borne impetuously forward like a crowd of triumphant feasters. Sit close down by it, and you see a fragment of the torrent against the sky, mottled, steely and foaming, leaping onward in far-flung criss-cross strands of water. Perpetually the eye is on the point of descrying a pattern in this weaving, and perpetually it is cheated by change. In one place part of the flood plunges over a ledge a few feet high and a quarter of a mile or so long, in a uniform and stable curve. It gives an impression of almost military concerted movement, grown suddenly out of confusion. But it is swiftly lost again in the multitudinous tossing merriment. Here and there a rock close to the surface is marked by a white wave that faces backwards and seems to be rushing madly upstream, but is really stationary in the headlong charge. But for these signs of reluctance, the waters seem to fling themselves on with some foreknowledge of their fate, in an even wilder frenzy. But it is no Maeterlinckian prescience. They prove, rather, that the great crashes are preceded by a louder merriment and a wilder gaiety. Leaping in the sunlight, careless, entwining, clamourously joyful, the waves riot on towards the verge.

But there they change. As they turn to the sheer descent, the white and blue and slate-colour, in the heart of the Canadian Falls at least, blend and deepen to rich wonderful, luminous green. On the edge of disaster the river seems to gather herself, to pause, to lift a head noble in ruin, and then, with a slow grandeur, to plunge into the eternal thunder and white chaos below. Where the stream runs shallower it is a kind of violet colour, but both violet and green fray and frill to white as they fall. The mass of water, striking some ever-hidden base of rock, leaps up the whole two hundred feet again in pinnacles and domes of spray. The spray falls back into the lower river once; all but a little that fines to foam and white mist, which drifts in layers along the air, graining it, and wanders out on the wind over the trees and gardens and houses, and so vanishes.'

The American side of the Falls, whose beauty, by comparison with the Canadian side, seemed to him 'almost delicate and fragile', made him realize, with heightened painterly perception, that on both sides

'the colour of the water is the ever-altering wonder. Greens and blues, purples and whites, melt into one another, fade, and come again, and change with the changing sun. Sometimes they are as richly diaphanous as a precious stone, and glow from within with a deep, inexplicable light. Sometimes the white intricacies of dropping foam become opaque and creamy. And always there are the rainbows. If you come suddenly upon the Falls from above, a great double rainbow, very vivid, spanning the extent of spray from top to bottom, is the first thing you see. If you wander along the cliff opposite, a bow springs into being in the American Falls, accompanies you courteously on your walk, dwindles and dies as the mist ends, and awakens again as you reach the Canadian tumult. And the bold traveller who attempts the trip under the American Falls sees, when he dare open his eyes to anything, tiny baby rainbows, some four or five yards in span, leaping from rock to rock among the foam, and gambolling beside him, barely out of hand's reach, as he goes. One I saw in that place was a complete circle, such as I have never seen before, and so near that I could put my foot on it. It is a terrifying journey, beneath and behind the Falls. The senses are battered and bewildered by the thunder of the water and the assault of wind and spray; or rather, the sound is not of falling water, but merely of falling; a noise of unspecified ruin.'

Amongst all these bravura descriptions of the North American natural scene it is good to come across Rupert's occasional sharp observations of people he encountered. As of the American Jewish businessman, whose 'mind was even more childlike and transparent than is usual with business men. The observer could see thoughts slowly floating into it, like carp in a pond. When they got near the surface, by a purely automatic process they found utterance. He was almost completely unconscious of an audience. Everything he thought of he said. He told me that his boots were giving in the sole, but would probably last this trip. He said he had not washed his feet for eight days; and that his clothes were shabby (which was true), but would do for Canada.' They were travelling to Quebec, and when they reached the city, which deeply impressed Rupert, they took a *calèche* together. Rupert fell into a reverie about the history of French Canada, but 'the reverie was broken by my friend struggling to his feet and standing, unsteady and bare-headed, in the swaying carriage. In that position he burst hoarsely into a song that I recognized as "The Star-Spangled Banner". We were passing the American Consulate. His song over, he settled down and fell into a deep sleep, and the *calèche* jolted down even narrower streets, curiously paved with planks, and ways that led through and under the ancient, tottering wooden houses.'

There was also 'a little old lady in black', in the chair next to his on the steamer that took them across Lake Superior. She 'kept a small telescope glued to her eye, hour after hour. Whenever she distinguished life on any shore we passed, she waved a tiny handkerchief. Diligently she did this, and with grave face, never visible to the objects of her devotion, I suppose, but certainly very happy; the most persistent lover of humanity I have ever seen. . . .'

Rupert devoted the last but one of his articles for the *Westminster Gazette* to the Indians. He was impressed by them, and touched, as a race still entirely different from the other Canadians who surrounded and had all but submerged them.

'Most tribes were very healthy, and some fine-looking. Such were the remarkable people who hunted, fought, feasted, and lived here until the light came, and all was changed. Other qualities they had even more remarkable to a European, such as utter honesty, and complete devotion to the truth among themselves. Civilization, disease, alcohol, and vice have reduced them to a few scattered communities and some stragglers, and a legend, the admiration of boyhood. . . . Some of the men, especially the older ones, have wonderful dignity and beauty of face and body. Their physique is superb; their features shaped and lined by weather and experience into a Roman nobility that demands respect. . . . What will happen? Will they be entirely swallowed by that ugliness of shops and trousers with which we enchain the earth, and become a memory and less than a memory? They are that already. The Indians have passed. They left no arts, no tradition, no buildings or roads or laws; only a story or two, and a few names, strange and beautiful.'

During his travels across North America, he was continually meeting literary people, editors, poets and critics, and was especially interested by the younger people at the universities with their eagerness for experiment in the theatre. Everywhere he went those who met him seem to have been struck, if not overwhelmed, by his looks. 'A young man more beautiful than he I had never seen,' wrote Ellery Sedgwick, editor of the *Atlantic Monthly* in Boston. 'Tall beyond the common, his loose tweeds accentuated his height and the athletic grace of his walk. His complexion was as ruddy as a young David's. His auburn hair rippled back from the central parting, careless but perfect. . . . Man's beauty is much more rare than woman's. I went home under the spell of it and at the foot of the stairs cried aloud to my wife, "I have seen Shelley plain!" ' R. H. Hathaway, a member of the Toronto Arts and Letters club, thought that he looked 'the veritable picture of a young Greek God, of Apollo himself', and like so many others before him in England, noticed the contrast between his finely athletic and virile general appearance and his delicate pink-and-white complexion, 'the colouring of a girl'.

His letters to Edward Marsh reveal that in the midst of the hurly-burly of meeting new people, the continual journeys from place to place, and his adventures into the wilder parts of the continent outside the cities, he had time to feel twinges of nostalgia for all he had left behind him. He sent Marsh a verse, reminding him of the happy party they had attended on Violet Asquith's birthday, which perhaps more than he could have realized sums up the change in his social milieu since the break with Bloomsbury:

> Would God I were eating plovers' eggs,
>   And drinking dry champagne,
> With the Bernard Shaws, Mr. & Mrs. Masefield,

Lady Horner, Neil Primrose, Raleigh, the Right
Honourable Augustine Birrell, Eddie, six or
Seven Asquiths, and Felicity Tree,
    In Downing Street again.

He continued to write long letters to Cathleen Nesbitt, and,
most difficult task of all, struggled to write what he intended
to be a definitive farewell letter to Ka. Guilt was painfully
mixed with the vestiges of his once-passionate feelings for her,
but at least he saw quite clearly that the break must be final.
He started his letter on board the *Cedric*, but failed to complete
it before they docked. Almost every night he dreamed of her.
He was afraid of going on with the letter because it made him
think too much about her, and all the old nightmare tangle of
feelings rose up again. He wrote the last page only after his
visit to Boston and Harvard, and posted it in New York on
25 June, almost a month after he had landed:

'You *must* get right clear of me, cease to love me, love and
marry somebody – and somebody worthy of you.

Oh my dear, let's try together to put things right. It's so
hard to know what to do – one's so stupid and blind and
blundering.

What I feel about you is this – I'm not arguing if it's true,
I just state it as it comes to my heart – "Ka is more precious
than anything. She has marvellous goodness and greatness in
her. She has things so lovely it hurts to name them. She is
greater and better, potentially, than any woman I know: and
more woman. She is very blind, and infinitely easy to lead
astray. Her goodness makes her a prey. She needs looking
after more than anybody else in the world. She's a lovely
child."

And with that in my heart I have to leave you. It's very
difficult. Oh Ka, you don't know how difficult it is! So have
pity on me. And forgive my breaking out like this. . . .

Dear child, dearest Ka, whom I've loved and known, you
must get well and happy, and live the great life you can. It's
the only thing I care for. Oh, child, I know I've done you
great wrong. What could I do? It was so difficult. You had
driven me mad.

I'm sorry for the wrong. It's the only thing in the world

I'm sorry for: though I've done a lot of evil things.
    I can't bear it that it is I have hurt you. . . .'

He told her that he still had a present to give her, a statuette
of a mother and child by Eric Gill, which Marsh was keeping
for him, and would send on to her as soon as he had an address
in England (she was still in Eastern Europe), 'because you'll be
the greatest mother in the world'. He promised her that, though
he had to leave her, he would always come to her help in an
emergency if she needed him. He ended the letter:

'I'm very happy and well, travelling. And in the end I'll get
back and work. Don't think of me.

    Please, Ka, be good and happy: and stick to and be
helped by your friends. That's the last thing I ask.

    This is so bad a letter: and I wanted to make everything
clear. Do believe. See what I've tried to write.

    Preaching and everything aside, let's just be Ka and Rupert
for a minute: and say goodbye so. I'll be loyal to the things
we've learnt together: and you be loyal. And life'll be good.
Dear love, goodbye.'

He had also told her that he wouldn't be writing again, and
as far as we know he sent her no further letter during the rest
of his travels. When they met again, briefly, after his return,
as far as he was concerned the fire had gone out. And yet there
were embers still under the ashes, and would be for the rest of
his life.

Peace Among the Islands

Rupert had crossed the whole of Canada from East to West by the beginning of September 1913, ending up in Vancouver Island. From there he took a boat back into the United States, and from Seattle went by train past the Coast Range to San Francisco, a city which he immediately liked and where he was much fêted. He was still restless, in spite of his bouts of nostalgia, and suddenly took the decision to travel on to the South Seas – the idea had been at the back of his mind for some time. He telegraphed to the ever-generous Loines for a loan of 250 dollars, which duly arrived. On 7 October he left in the s.s. *Sierra* for Honolulu.

Rupert's Pacific journey took him from Hawaii to Samoa and then to Fiji, on for a short visit to New Zealand, and thence at the beginning of January 1914 to Tahiti where he lingered until April. The ostensible reason for the lingering was a leg poisoned by wounds when he grazed it against a coral reef, but he was in no hurry to move. He was happy in spite of the lameness, not only because he had fallen in love with Tahiti – it was the culmination of a love affair with the South Sea islands which had been growing ever since he landed in Hawaii – but also because he had formed a deep attachement to a native girl at Mataia, whom he was to call Mamua in his poem *Tiare Tahiti*.

Only one public piece of writing about the South Seas appeared during his lifetime. It was chiefly on Samoa, and he called it *Some Niggers*, because an American Suffragist lady on board the ship which took him to Pago-Pago exclaimed, as they approached the harbour, 'Look at those niggers! Whose are they?' It was included in the 1916 volume *Letters from America*, but was originally contributed to the *New Statesman* and not to the *Westminster Gazette*. Like his earlier articles,

Some Niggers is full of sharp observation and imaginative descriptive writing which vividly conveys the spell the South Sea islands laid on him :

> 'They are composed, these islands, of all legendary heavens. They are Calypso's and Prospero's isle, and the Hesperides and Paradise, and every timeless and untroubled spot. Such tales have been made of them by men who have been there, and gone away, and have been haunted by the smell of the bush and the lagoons, and faint thunder on the distant reef, and the colours of sky and sea and coral, and the beauty and grace of the islanders. And the queer thing is that it's all, almost tiresomely, true. In the South Seas the Creator seems to have laid himself out to show what He *can* do. Imagine an island with the most perfect climate in the world, tropical, yet almost always cooled by a breeze from the sea. No malaria or other fevers. No dangerous beasts, snakes or insects. Fish for the catching, and fruits for plucking. And an earth and sky and sea of immortal loveliness. What more could civilization give? Umbrellas? Rope? Gladstone bags?... Any one of the vast leaves of the banana is more waterproof than the most expensive woven stuff. And from the first tree you can tear off a long strip of fibre that holds better than any rope. And thirty seconds' work on a great palm-leaf produces a basket-bag which will carry incredible weights all day, and can be thrown away in the evening. A world of conveniences. And the things which civilization has left behind or missed by the way are there, too, among the Polynesians: beauty and courtesy and mirth I think there is no gift of mind or body that the wise value which these people lack. A man I met in some other islands, who had travelled much all over the world, said to me, "I have found no man, in or out of Europe, with the good manners and dignity of the Samoan, with the possible exception of the Irish peasant. A people among whom an Italian would be uncouth, and a high-caste Hindu-vulgar, and Karsavina would seem clumsy, and Helen of Troy a frump." '

Rupert had evidently prepared this article before war broke out, though at the end he mentions that the New Zealanders had just captured Samoa and ousted the Germans. He had praise for German colonial rule in the island group, the chief

characteristic of which seemed to him to have been leaving
the islanders as far as possible to go their own ways within a
fair and efficient administrative framework; but at the same
time he records instances of Samoan hostility to the Germans
and an eagerness for the men of Peritania (Britain) to take over
their protection. He concludes his article on a clearly more
personal note, an eloquent evocation which is almost rhapsody
to the profound alteration of values he felt to be taking place
in his whole being, as he sank himself into the atmosphere of
the place:

> 'It is a magic of a different way of life. In the South Seas,
> if you live the South Sea life, the intellect soon lapses into
> quiescence. The body becomes more active, the senses and
> perceptions more lordly and acute. It is a life of swimming
> and climbing and resting after exertion. The skin seems to
> grow more sensitive to light and air, and the feel of water
> and the earth and leaves. Hour after hour one may float in
> the warm lagoons, conscious, in the whole body, of every
> shred and current of the multitudinous water, or diving under
> in a vain attempt to catch the radiant butterfly-coloured
> fish that flit in and out of the thousand windows of their
> gorgeous coral palaces. Or go up, one of a singing flower-
> garlanded crowd, to a shaded pool of a river in the bush,
> cool from the mountains. The blossom-hung darkness is
> streaked with the bodies that fling themselves, head or feet
> first, from the cliffs around the water, and the haunted
> forest-silence is broken by laughter. It is part of the charm
> of these people that, while they are not so foolish as to
> "think", their intelligence is incredibly lively and subtle,
> their sense of humour and their intuitions of other people's
> feelings are very keen and living. They have built up, in the
> long centuries of their civilization, a delicate and noble
> complexity of behaviour and personal relationships. A white
> man living with them soon feels his mind as deplorably dull
> as his skin is pale and unhealthy among those glorious golden-
> brown bodies. But even he soon learns to *be* his body (and
> so his true mind), instead of using it as a stupid convenience
> for his personality, a moment's umbrella against this world.
> He is perpetually and intensely aware of the subtleties of
> taste in food, of every tint and line of the incomparable

glories of those dawns and evenings, of each shade of intercourse in fishing or swimming or dancing with the best
companions in the world. That alone is life; all else is death.
And after dark, the black palms against a tropic night, the
smell of the wind, the tangible moonlight like a white, dry,
translucent mist, the lights in the huts, the murmur and
laughter of passing figures, the passionate, queer thrill of the
rhythm of some hidden dance – all this will seem to him,
inexplicably and almost unbearably, a scene his heart has
known long ago, and forgotten, and yet always looked for.'

In default of further articles, his letters home are an eloquent
indication of the magic web the islands wove about him. They
are also, in general, less self-conscious and less flippant than had
been characteristic previously, and full of picturesque and
amusing detail. They recall those other letters from abroad, a
poet to his more prosaic friend in England, Shelley in the blazing
discovery of Italy to Peacock – though they show a greater sense
of humour. To Cathleen Nesbitt he wrote, at the beginning of
November, when he was about to embark for Fiji from Samoa:

'The sea made me stupider and stupider: and I found I
couldn't get a letter to you till God knows when. And here
I am in Samoa: I left the *Ventura*, my boat, at Pango-Pango,
which is the port in the American island of this group. The
loveliest little harbour in the world: great hills covered with
thick forests all round, and a little lake of blue in the middle,
and a queer air of tropics over all, and the loveliest people
in coloured loin cloths trotting round. I went for a walk
under the coconut palms, with a naked baby of five or six
holding each hand (one said his name was *Fred*), and several
more twining round my ankles. I had a coco-nut – for it was
hot – in the house of a white trader who had married a native.
Have you ever sent a chocolate-coloured youth up an immense
almost perpendicular coco-nut palm to pick a baby coco-nut,
and then drunk the milk? It is the most refreshing thing in
the world, on such an occasion.

In the evening, the wharf was covered with torches, lamps,
and a mass of Samoans, all with some "curios" or other on
little stalls. The sailors and passengers from the ship wandered
among them buying or bartering. The Samoans were rather
indifferent about money, but would give anything they had

for old clothes. Great bronze men, with gilded hair, and godlike limbs lay about on the grass, while their women held up pieces of "kapa" – which is bark beaten into a stiff cloth, and covered with a brown pattern – and grinned and beckoned and gesticulated. And the whole was lit up by these flaring lights against the tropical nights and the palms and stars, so that it looked like a Rembrandt picture – you know those things where there's a light on the immediate figures and faces, and the rest are in inky darkness? After dinner six girls and six men came on board and performed a *siva-siva* on deck, before the astonished eyes of the American and Australian passengers. . . .'

To Marsh, on his way to Fiji, he broke out:

'Oh, Eddie, it's all true about the South Seas! I get a little tired of it at moments, because I am just too old for Romance, & my soul is seared. But there it is: there it wonderfully is: heaven on earth, the ideal life, little work, dancing singing & eating, naked people of incredible loveliness, perfect manners, & immense kindliness, a divine tropic climate, & intoxicating beauty of scenery. . . . And, Eddie, it's all true about, for instance, coconuts. You tramp through a strange vast dripping tropical forest for hours, listening to weird liquid hootings from birds and demons in the branches above. Then you feel thirsty. So you send your boy – or call a native – up a great perpendicular palm. He runs up with utter ease & grace, cuts off a couple of vast nuts & comes down & makes holes in them. And they're chock-full of the best drink in the world. Romance! Romance! I walked 15 miles through mud & up & down mountains, & swam three rivers, to get this boat. But if you ever miss me, suddenly, one day, from lecture-room B in King's, or from the Moulin d'Or at lunch, you'll know that I've got sick for the full moon on these little thatched roofs, & the palms against the morning, & Samoan boys & girls diving thirty feet into a green sea or a deep mountain pool under a waterfall – & that I've gone back.'

And to Edmund Gosse, when he had arrived in Fiji:

'Perplexing country! At home everything is so simple, and choice is swift, for the sensible man. There is only the choice between writing a good sonnet and making a million pounds. Who could hesitate? But *here* the choice is between writing a sonnet and climbing a straight hundred-foot coco-nut palm, or diving forty feet from a rock into pellucid blue-green water. Which is the better, there? One's European literary soul begins to be haunted by strange doubts and shaken with fundamental fantastic misgivings. I think I shall return home. . . . The idea of the South Seas as a place of passion and a Mohammedan's paradise is but a sailor's yarn. It is nothing near so disturbing. It is rather the opposite to alcohol, according to the Porter's definition [in *Macbeth*]; for it promotes performance but takes away desire. Yet I can even understand Stevenson finding – as you put it – the Shorter Catechism there. One keeps realizing, however unwillingly, responsibility. I noticed in myself and in the other white people in Samoa, a trait I have remarked in schoolmasters and in the "agents" who are appointed in Canada to live with, and look after, the Indians. You know that sort of slightly irritated tolerance, a lack of *ir*responsibility, that mark the pedagogue? One feels that one's a White Man – ludicrously. I kept thinking I was in the Sixth at Rugby again. These dear good people, with their laughter and friendliness and crowns of flowers – one feels one *must* protect them.'

The two young native bearers who went with him in his explorations of Fiji, he speaks of in his letters almost in terms of a love-affair. He described them to Cathleen Nesbitt:

'The two "boys" (aged 23 or 4), I took with me when I went walking through the centre of the island, to carry my bags, are my sworn and eternal friends. One of them ("Ambele", under which I, but not you, can recognize "Abel") was six foot high, very broad, and more perfectly made than any man or statue I have ever seen. His grin stretched from ear to ear. And he could carry me across rivers (when I was tired of swimming them, for we crossed vast rivers every mile or two) for a hundred yards or so, as I should carry a box of matches. I think of bringing him back with me as a servant and bodyguard to England. He loved me because though I was far weaker than he, I was far braver. The Fijians are rather cowards. And on precipices I am peculiarly reckless. The boys saved me from rolling off to perdition about thirty times – and respected me for it – though thinking me insane. Would you marry me if I turned up with two vast cannibal servants black-skinned and perpetually laughing all of us attired only in loincloths and red flowers in our hair? I think I should be irresistible.'

About the cannibal past of the Fijians he wrote in black humour, with a sudden and even more violent attack of his old desire to shock, to Violet Asquith, a letter one cannot be sure she appreciated:

'It's twenty years since they've eaten anybody in this part of Fiji, and far more since they've done what I particularly and unreasonably detest – fastened the victim down, cut pieces off him one by one, and cooked and eaten them before his eyes. To witness one's own transubtantiation into a naked black man, that seems the last indignity. Consideration of the thoughts that pour through the mind of the ever-diminishing remnant of a man, as it sees its last limbs cooking, moves me deeply. I have been meditating a sonnet, as I sit here, surrounded by dusky faces and gleaming eyes: Dear, they have poached the eyes you loved so well. It'd do well for No. 101 and last, in a modern sonnet-sequence, wouldn't it? I don't know how it would go on. The fourth line would have to be "And all my turbulent lips are *maître-d'hotel*" – I don't know how to scan French, I fancy that limps. But *all* is very strong in the modern style. . . .'

He continued with an equally macabre sonnet in octosyllabics, but then went back with scarcely a break to a rhapsody about his surroundings – untainted by reflection about what might have been happening twenty years before:

'Fiji in moonlight is like nothing else in this life or the next. It is all dim colours and all scents. And here, where it's high up, the most fantastically shaped mountains in the world tower up all around, and little silver clouds and wisps of mist run bleating up and down the valleys and hill-sides like lambs looking for their mother. There's only one thing on earth as beautiful: & that's Samoa by night. That's utterly different, merely Heaven, sheer loveliness. You lie on a mat in a cool Samoan hut and look out on the white sand under the high palms, and a gentle sea, & the black line of the reef a mile out & moonlight over everything, floods and floods of it, not sticky, like Honolulu moonlight, not to be eaten with a spoon, but flat and abundant, such that you could slice thin golden-white shavings off it, as off cheese . . . and among it all are the loveliest people in the world, moving and running and dancing like gods and goddesses, very quietly and mysteriously, and utterly content. It's sheer beauty, so pure that it's difficult to breathe in it – like living in a Keats world, only it's less syrupy. Endymion without sugar. Completely unconnected with this world . . . I continue in a hot noon, under an orange tree. We rose at dawn and walked many miles and swam seven large rivers and picked and ate many oranges and pine-apples and drank coco-nuts. Now the two "boys" who carry my luggage are asleep in the shade. . . .'

In spite of revelling in these South Sea paradises, he was sometimes assailed by nostalgic thoughts of what he had left behind, what he wanted to revive the moment he got back to England. To Jacques Raverat, on 1 December 1913, he wrote:

'I know what things are good: friendship and work and conversation. These I shall have. How one can fill life, if one's energetic, and knows how to dig! I have thought of a thousand things to do, in books and poems and plays and theatres and societies and housebuilding and dinner-parties when I get Home. Ho, but we shall have fun. . . . There is no man who has had such friends as I, so many, so fine, so various, so multiform, so prone to laughter, so strong in affection and so permanent, so trustworthy, so courteous, so stern with vices, and so blind to faults or folly, of such swiftness of mind and strength of body, so polypist (= of many faiths, *not* bespattered by a parrot, O Greekless!) and yet benevolent, and so apt both to make jokes and to understand them. Also, their faces are beautiful, and I love them. I repeat a very long list of their names, every night before I sleep. Friendship is always exciting and yet always safe. There is no lust in it, and therefore no poison. It is cleaner than love, and older; for children and very old people have friends, but they do not love. It gives more and takes less, it is fine in the enjoying, and without pain when absent, and it leaves only good memories. In love all laughter ends with an ache, but laughter is the very garland on the head of friendship. I will not love, and I will not be loved. But I will have friends round me continually, all the days of my life, and in whatever lands I may be.'

It is, I think, to be noted that Rupert's deep-seated puritan suspicion of physical love rears its head again here, a revulsion that had been in the darkness of his mind ever since the crisis with Ka. It is nevertheless ironical that he should make this declaration on the eve of what has every appearance of having been the only perfect and surely consummated love-affair of his life. He reached Tahiti from New Zealand at the end of January 1914, and realized that he had at last landed in 'the most ideal place in the world'. He stayed there much longer than he originally planned, more than three months in fact, partly because he was again, as in Fiji, suffering from blood poisoning in his legs, due to scratching them on coral and not looking after the wounds properly, partly because his funds were running very low again, but above all because he had fallen in love with a native girl called Taata (or Tuata) Mata, to whom, calling her Mamua, he addressed one of his best poems of this period – which is also one of the most successful 'sentimental' poems he ever composed, avoiding the faults which marred so many of his earlier poems in the same vein. Rupert was always at his best in his poetry when lightheartedness was a dominant element – as in *Grantchester*. In this poem to Taata he used his now favourite octosyllabics, as Shelley did in his love lyrics to Jane Williams, the mood of which it cannot fail to recall, even more than Marvell's octosyllabics:

> Mamua, when our laughter ends,
> And hearts and bodies, brown as white,
> Are dust about the doors of friends,
> Or scent a-blowing down the night,
> Then, oh! then, the wise agree,
> Comes our immortality.
> Mamua, there waits a land
> Hard for us to understand.
> Out of time, beyond the sun,
> All are one in Paradise,
> You and Pupure are one,
> And Taü, and the ungainly wise.
> There the Eternals are, and there

The Good, the Lovely and the True,
And Types, whose earthly copies were
The foolish broken things we knew. . . .
Oh, Heaven's Heaven! – but we'll be missing
The palms, and sunlight, and the south;
And there's an end, I think, of kissing,
When our mouths are one with Mouth. . . .

    Taü here, Mamua,
Crown the hair, and come away!
Hear the calling of the moon,
And the whispering scents that stray
About the idle warm lagoon.
Hasten, hand in human hand,
Down the dark, the flowered way,
Along the whiteness of the sand,
And in the water's soft caress,
Wash the mind of foolishness,
Mamua, until the day.
Spend the glittering moonlight there
Pursuing down the soundless deep
Limbs that gleam and shadowy hair,
Or floating lazy, half-asleep.
Dive and double and follow after,
Snare in flowers, and kiss, and call,
With lips that fade, and human laughter
And faces individual,
Well this side of Paradise! . . .
There's little comfort in the wise.

In relation to this playing so happily with Platonic ideas,
some observations of Walter de la Mare, when he tried to
define the particular nature of Rupert's poetry in his acutely
perceptive essay 'Rupert Brooke and the Intellectual Imagination', seem especially pertinent:

'The visionaries, those whose eyes are fixed on the distance,
on the beginning and the end, rather than the incident and
excitement, of life's journey, have to learn to substantiate
their imaginings, to base their fantastic palaces on terra firma,
to weave their dreams into the fabric of actuality. But the
source and origin of their poetry is in the world within. The

intellectual imagination, on the other hand, flourishes on knowledge and experience. It must first explore before it can analyse, devour before it can digest, the world in which it finds itself. It feeds and feeds upon ideas, but because it is creative, it expresses them in terms of humanity, of the senses and the emotions, makes life of them, that is. There is less mystery, less magic in its poetry. It does not demand of its reader so profound or so complete a surrender. But if any youthfulness is left in us, we can share its courage, enthusiasm and energy, its zest and enterprise, its penetrating thought, its wit, fevour, passion, and we should not find it impossible to sympathize with its wild revulsions of faith and feeling, its creative scepticism.'

In his letter to Marsh of 7 March, Rupert wrote: 'I have been nursed & waited on by a girl with wonderful eyes, the walk of a goddess, & the heart of an angel, who is, luckily, devoted to me. She gives her time to ministering to me, I mine to probing her queer mind. I think I shall write a book about her – Only I fear I'm too fond of her.' On his arrival in San Francisco his thoughts were still of her, as he wrote in another letter to Marsh: 'How I hate civilization & houses & trams and collars. If I got on the *Tahiti* & went back again, shouldn't I find a quay covered with moving lights & lovely forms in white & pink & scarlet & green? And wouldn't Taata Mata be waiting there to welcome me with wide arms?' At the same time his mind, turning England-wards, was suddenly filled with moody thoughts that included some of his least admirable obsessions: 'It'll be good,' he wrote to the Cornfords (his letter was in fact addressed in fun to their daughter Helena, who was only six months old) from the *Tahiti*,

'to get back to theatres and supper parties & arguments & hedges & roast beef & misty half-colours. But oh! sometimes – I warn you – I'll be having Samoan or Tahitian "thoughts". When everything's *too* grey, & there's an amber fog that bites your throat, & everyone's irritable and in a high state of nerves, & the pavement's greasy, and London is full of "Miles of shopping women, served by men", and another Jew has bought a peerage, and I've a cold in my nose, and the ways are full of lean & vicious people, dirty, hermaphrodites and eunuchs, Stracheys, moral vagabonds, pitiable scum – why, then I shall have a *Sudseegedenke*, a thought of 20° South, a Samoan thought. . . .'

Taata Mata continued to haunt him. In writing to Dudley Ward from the R.N. Camp near Blandford much later, in December 1914, he described a nightmarish dream he had just had:

'Last night I rolled about in this so-called bed. I've been bad lately with inoculation, a cough and things. And I dreamt I landed at Papeete, and went up between the houses, and the air was heavy with sunshine. I went into the house of a half-caste woman I know and she gave me tea, and talked. And she told me about everyone. And at last I said "And how and where's Taata Mata?" And she said "Oh – didn't you know?" And I said "No". She said "She's dead". I asked (knowing the answer) "When did she die?" "Months ago, just after you left." She kept evading my eye. After a long silence I asked (feeling very sick) "Did she kill herself?" The half-caste nodded. I went out of the house and out to the lagoon, feeling that a great friendliness – all the place – had gone against me. Then I woke with a dry throat, and found a frosty full moon blazing in at the window, and the bugle hammering away at the 6.30 *Reveille*. Perhaps it was the full moon made me dream, because of the last full moon at Mataia (about which there is an unfinished poem: now in German possession). Perhaps it was my evil heart. I think the dream was true. "There is no health in me" as we used to say in some Confession in Chapel. And now I'm not only sicker with myself than ever: but also I've got another bad attack of *Heimweh* for the South Seas.'

Only a month later, he received a long-delayed letter from Taata Mata, which was dated 14 May. It had been recovered from the wreck of the *Empress of Ireland*. 'I just wrote you some lines about Tahiti today,' she wrote, describing a visit of a party of Argentinians to her island, during which 'all girls in Papeete have good time with Argentin boys.' She went on in a mixture of pidgin English and French: 'I wish you here that might I get fat all time Sweetheart you know I always thinking about you that time when you left me I been sorry for long time. We have good time when you was here I always

remember about you forget me all readly oh! mon cher bien
aime je t'aimerai toujours . . . je me rappeler toujours votre
petite etroite figure et la petite bouche que me baise bien tu
m'a percea mon coeur et j'aime toujours ne m'oubli pas mon
cher. . . .' She ended: 'I send you my kiss to you darling – mille
kiss.'

As far as we know this was the only communication he ever
received from Taata Mata. But in spite of the months that had
elapsed between the date of the letter and his dream, it seems
to have made Rupert believe that his dream was wrong and that
she was still alive. In his last letter of instructions to Dudley
Ward, when he was dying, and knew he was dying, he wrote:
'Try to inform Taata of my death. Mlle. Taata, Hotel Tiare,
Papete, Tahiti. It might find her. Give her my love.'

11

The Observed of All Observers

On his way home across America at the end of April he stopped off at Chicago. He had a note of introduction in his pocket from Harold Monro to Maurice Browne, director of the Chicago Little Theater, and his wife, the actress Ellen von Volkenburg. They quickly found that they were kindred spirits. Maurice Browne introduced him to many of his friends, all of whom seemed to have been stunned by his beauty, with his hair now more bleached gold than red after the sunshine of the South Seas. He was the 'observed of all observers', and everyone turned round in the streets. For three nights they talked, argued, sang songs and read aloud. Among the things they read aloud were Rupert's new poems written in Tahiti, and also his play *Lithuania*.

Rupert had written *Lithuania* when staying in a pension near his friend Dudley Ward during his first visit to Germany in the spring of 1912, where he also wrote *Grantchester*. It is in some ways the most curious of Rupert's productions, and shows, one must admit, little more than a slight gift for *Grand Guignol*; certainly no promise that the author might have gone on to write full-length plays of a more serious sort. An acquaintance of Ward's had one day told him of a macabre incident that had taken place in some village in Lithuania. A boy had left home when he was thirteen years old, and no news of him ever reached his family. One morning, years later, he came back, pretending to be only a traveller looking for shelter for the night. They found him a bed: his plan was to spring a great surprise on them the next morning, revealing that he was the long-lost son, with a wallet stuffed with money for them, and a gold watch. The sight of the watch aroused the greed of the parents, who persuaded his sister to murder him during the night. The man had not, however, been so secretive to some of the other villagers, and one of them came round the next morning to congratulate the family on the unexpected and happy occurrence. That is the grim end of the playlet. It was never put on in England during Brooke's lifetime – it only ran for half an hour – but Maurice Browne bravely produced it at his Little Theatre in 1913.

One of the first people Rupert Brooke met after his return to England in June 1914 was a 'small, dark, shy man, with spectacles and straight, slightly greasy-looking hair' (as Maurice Browne described him), with 'a queer little green hat which tipped up preposterously in front'. This was Lascelles Abercrombie, one of his fellow-contributors to *Georgian Poetry*, to whom he was to become closely attached as poetic colleague in this last year of his life, and whom he was to make one of his three literary heirs, with Walter de la Mare and Wilfred Gibson. 'I think he's very remarkable,' Rupert observed in a letter to Ka directly afterwards. 'He laughs very well.'

While Rupert was away on his travels, Abercrombie had founded, together with Gibson, a poetry magazine called *New Numbers*, published from his home at Ryton, near Dymock in Gloucestershire. It was originally to be called *The Gallows Garland*, from the name of his cottage, *The Gallows*, which gruesomely commemorated the hanging of a highwayman at its front door. The news reached Rupert, who was immediately enthusiastic to be associated with it, and, employing Marsh as his intermediary, sent the editors new poems from the South Seas as he finished them. From Rugby at the beginning of July he wrote to Russell Loines: 'You will have received from Wilfred Gibson a parcel of *New Numbers*, as you demanded. The thing is going pretty well: about seven or eight hundred of each number, which pays expenses very easily, and leaves a good bit for division. It goes on selling steadily, & I suppose it always will – I mean the back numbers will continue to go off. I hope so, for the more it's sold, the more poetry, & less reviews, Abercrombie and Gibson can write: & the better for the world.' Rupert's war sonnets were first published in its last issue: so great was the public demand that the editors were forced to use up all the paper they had been able to get hold of under wartime conditions, and closed down.

It is interesting to note that Abercrombie and Gibson (who

lived not far off from Abercrombie on the other side of Dymock) persuaded the American poet Robert Frost to take a house near them during the early months of 1914, and published several of his poems in *New Numbers*. And it was after a visit to this idyllic poets' retreat in Gloucestershire that Marsh definitely decided to follow his first volume of *Georgian Poetry* with a second selection. It is uncertain whether it had always been at the back of his mind to make a series of *Georgian Poetry*; but the immense success of the first volume provided the strongest of arguments now for him to try his hand again. No doubt Abercrombie and Gibson discussed it eagerly with him during his visit, and managed to overcome any remaining hesitation he may have had. The two poets, it seems, also urged him to include poems by Frost; but Marsh eventually decided against it, on the grounds that the work of an American poet, however closely in sympathy with his British contributors, would interfere with the overall pattern (though he had asked Pound to be represented in the first volume). The selection was all but ready by the early summer, but the outbreak of war caused the whole plan to be dropped for the time being; and it was not till 1915, after Rupert's death, that *Georgian Poetry 1913–15* finally appeared. It is possible that Rupert himself still had some irritated reservations about Marsh's uncompromising editorial role, because in the same letter to Loines I have quoted above, he wrote: 'I'm also sending a package which explains itself: "Georgian Drawings". . . . It's generally agreed that Marsh has got Georgianism on the brain, & will shortly issue a series of Georgian poker-work: & establish a band of Georgian cooks.'

In his Prefatory Note to this second volume Marsh showed that he had taken to heart some of the criticisms of the first. He wrote: 'A few of the contributors to the former volume are not represented in this one, either because they have published nothing that comes within its scope, or because they belong in fact to an earlier poetic generation, and their inclusion must be allowed to have been an anachronism. Two names are added.' The excluded, who can hardly have relished being called 'an anachronism', were Chesterton, Sturge Moore, Ronald Ross, Sargant, and Trevelyan. Perhaps these were the 'rotters' Rupert had grumbled about. The two new names were Ralph Hodgson and Francis Ledwidge.

Rupert came back home as troubled as ever by his unmarried state, envying his married friends, and proclaiming at one moment that marriage was the only thing that mattered and at another that he was too old for it. The strange thing is that though he continued to write adoring letters to Cathleen Nesbitt he does not seem to have made any approach to her to marry him. From Washington, a last stop before catching the boat to England, he wrote excitedly to her on 14 May, announcing that he expected to arrive in Plymouth on 5 June: 'Carissima, I have dreamt of you. I want to see your face. Where you are, or what doing, I do not know: for I shall get my recent mail (D.V.) in New York tomorrow. I hope that you are well and happy. I know that you are beautiful. I am so tired of seeing people and going over buildings and observing "significant" phenomena. I desire to rest, and observe only what is significant to Eternity – you, that is. It is just a year – Dear child, in three weeks!'

Ka got to know that he was back, and in spite of his 'farewell' letter suggested a meeting: she could not get him out of her thoughts or dreams. He agreed, but warned her to avoid it if she was likely to be upset. They met in a tea-shop, but it must have been a tense occasion, because each wrote to the other afterwards, fearing that there might have been a backwash of misery or despair. Whether he had been, or was now, in communication with Noel we do not know.

Once more in London, Rupert plunged at once into his old round of luncheons and dinners and theatrical parties. He was constantly in the company of his new friends of the Asquith-Churchill circle, who liked at that time to patronize the arts and young artists and poets who had made their mark. He was invited to 10 Downing Street for a recital by Ruth Draper; and again a few days later for an evening with the Asquiths, during which his friend Denis Browne played the piano and Steuart Wilson, who had been with him at King's, sang; ten days later he was taken by Marsh to an even grander dinner at the house of the Duchess of Leeds, where for the first time he met Lady Eileen Wellesley, daughter of the Duke of Wellington, who was to become an intimate friend in the last phase of his life and recipient of many rather more than affectionate letters.

The first of these letters which we have is dated 'Rugby, Sunday night in bed, some time in July':

'Oh dear, I've been so busy all day: & I can't quite remember why. This morning – this morning I read the paper: & then thought about it: & then thought about other things: & then it was lunch. This afternoon my brother drove me out in the car. And now it's tonight.

We looked at all the places thirty miles away . . . Finally I chose Hampden-in-Arden. I remember once passing through a station of that name. And I've always wanted to see the forest of Arden . . . Hampden-in-Arden. What a name to dream about! Perhaps one shouldn't have *gone* there. Arden – it's ten miles north of Stratford – is a little tamed nowadays. No holly & horns & shepherds & dukes. We caught one glimpse of a hart weeping large-eyed on the brink of the Stratford-Birmingham canal. Neither Rosalind nor Audrey. And Orlando's in an O.T.C. on Salisbury Plain. Everyone else was Jaques: I a shadowy Touchstone. . . .

Hampden was just full of the plutocracy of Birmingham, short, crafty, proudly vulgar men, for all the world like heroes of Arnold Bennett's novels. They were extraordinarily dressed, for the most part in very expensive clothes, but without collars. I think they'd *started* in collars, but removed them by the way. They rolled out of their cars, and along the street, none so much as five foot high, all hot, & canny to the point of unintelligibility, emitting the words "Eh . . ." or "Ah, lad . . ." at intervals. They were profound, terrifying, and of the essence of Life: but unlovely. But in Richmond Park there's you. It's too late. I must go to sleep. God be with you. You frightened me by coughing up a red stain in the cab. You're all right, aren't you? Please take care of yourself. Eileen, there's something solid & real & wonderful about you, in a world of shadows. Do you know how real you are? The time with you is the only waking hours in a life of dreams. All that's another way of saying I adore you.

Goodnight. Rupert.'

After the dinner at the Duchess of Leeds', a group of the guests went over to Sir Ian Hamilton's place in Hyde Park Gardens to see Marjorie Hamilton dance. Less than a year later Sir Ian was to be Rupert's Commander-in-Chief on the Gallipoli expedition. There was a reunion of the Apostles at the Connaught Rooms, at which James Strachey appears to have been present. Rupert appears to have re-established some kind of *modus vivendi* with him after his return, but the ghost of Lulworth had not been laid. In July they spent what appeared to James to be a very happy evening together at the Hippodrome; but there must have been some discussion of Lytton again, because directly afterwards Rupert wrote him a curt note to say that his (James's) opinions were intolerable to him. It was the last letter he ever wrote to James, the most steadfast, devoted, and once so well-loved friend of his early youth.

There were more lunches at the favourite Moulin d'Or, at one of which he met the artist Gaudier-Brzeska. He lunched with Henry James and Mrs Belloc-Lowndes, and attended a theatrical supper-party at the Savoy given by J. M. Barrie, with Marie Tempest, Gerald du Maurier, Granville-Barker, Shaw, Yeats and Chesterton as the other guests. Marsh outdid himself at this period in introducing his beloved Rupert to everyone he knew of influence, fame or promise. On 9 July he invited Paul Nash, W. H. Davies and Siegfried Sassoon to meet him over breakfast at Gray's Inn. Like everyone else among his new acquaintances, Sassoon fell for him at first encounter. Many years later, in *The Weald of Youth*, he wrote about this meeting, remarking on

> 'the almost meditative deliberation of his voice. His movements, too, so restful, so controlled, and so unaffected. But beyond that was my assured perception that I was in the presence of one on whom had been conferred all the invisible attributes of a poet. To this his radiant good looks seemed subsidiary. Here, I might well have thought – had my divinations been expressible – was a being singled out for some transplendent performance, some enshrined achievement.'

12

An Unusual Young Man
Goes to War

The outbreak of war between the Central Powers and Russia found Rupert at home in Rugby. The evening before Marsh had taken him to dine again at No. 10, where he sat between Asquith and his daughter Violet. Winston Churchill, First Lord of the Admiralty, whom he had not met before, was also at the dinner and offered to help him to get a commission if the war, as seemed most likely, soon involved Britain. The confusion of his feelings is shown by his letter to Jacques Raverat that evening:

'Everyone in the governing classes seems to think we shall all be at war.

Everything's just the wrong way round. *I* want Germany to smash Russia to fragments, and then France to break Germany. Instead of which I'm afraid Germany will badly smash France, and then be wiped out by Russia. France and England are the only countries that ought to have any power. Prussia is a devil. And Russia means the end of Europe and any decency.

I suppose the future is a Slav Empire, world-wide, despotic, and insane.'

To Lady Eileen Wellesley he wrote: 'If war comes, should one enlist? Or turn war correspondent? Or what?' He had gone to Cley-next-the-sea in Norfolk to be with the Cornfords directly after his twenty-seventh birthday celebrations in Rugby, and it was there that he heard that Britain was at war. He was full of the darkest foreboding, and knew in his heart that not only the Army and Navy, but soon everyone else would be involved in the fighting. His first aim was to get taken on as a War Correspondent, but he found his way blocked. He

explored the chances of 'volunteering', but found that way
blocked too, at any rate for his impatient aims. He wrote to
Jacques Raverat on the 6th: 'One can't "go and fight" in
England. Volunteers are admitted neither to the Navy nor the
Army. If one joins the Territorials now, they give you six
months' training, and then let you garrison the chief ports and
sea towns, *if* the Expeditionary Force leaves England. It *might*
be worth doing, *if* the Expeditionary Force *does* leave England.

Ten days later, still fretting and confused, he wrote again
to Lady Eileen:

> 'It's not so easy as you think – for a person who has no
> military training or knowledge, save the faint, almost
> pre-natal, remembrance of some khaki drilling at Rugby – to
> get to the "front". I'm one of a band who've been offering
> themselves, with vague persistence, to their country, in
> various quarters of London for some days, and being con-
> tinually refused. In time, one of the various doors we tap at
> will be opened. Meanwhile, I wander.
>
> One gets introspective. I find in myself two natures – not
> necessarily conflicting, but – different. There's half my heart
> which is normal & English – what's the word, not quite
> "good" or "honourable" – "straight", I think. But the other
> half is a wanderer and a solitary, selfish, unbound, and
> doubtful. Half my heart is of England, the rest is looking for
> some home I haven't yet found. . . .'

At the beginning of September he was still 'wandering'. He
had probably been seeing something, in the stress of the crisis,
of his old Bloomsbury friends, for he wrote to Cathleen Nesbitt,
who was on tour in the provinces, in a mood of continuing
revulsion, but even more extreme in his bitterness: 'One of
the less creditable periods of my life enmeshed me with the
intellectuals. I hover on their fringes yet: dehumanized, disgusting people. They are mostly pacifists and pro-Germans. I quarrel
with them twice a day.'

Nevertheless it must have been about this time that he wrote
for the *New Statesman* his article *An Unusual Young Man*. It
must be considered as a piece of disguised autobiography, and
reflects even more clearly the chaos of ambivalent feelings
which the outbreak of war stirred up in him. It purports to be
the ruminations of 'a friend of mine', 'a normal, even ordinary

young man, wholly English, twenty-four years old, active and given to music'. This young man stayed in Germany, in Munich and Berlin, and was haunted by the beauty of the places he had visited and the happy times he had had there, with his intimate friends and drinking companions. 'A thousand little figures tumbled through his mind. But they no longer brought with them that air of comfortable kindness which Germany had always signified for him.' As he reflects on the possibility of becoming a soldier and having to fight, he finds it hard to accept the idea of meeting his former friends as enemies in battle. Immediately after, he is overcome by the idea of England, above all its countryside, its 'holiness'. And yet his conclusion is still ambivalent, with a dubious note of resignation : 'Well, if Armageddon's *on*, I suppose one should be there. . . . He thought often and heavily of Germany. Of England, all the time. He didn't know whether he was glad or sad. It was a new feeling.' It was only after he had taken part in the Antwerp expedition, and seen the mass flight of the Belgian populace before the German advance, that Rupert became out-and-out anti-German. It does not appear that either his doubts or his final patriotic convictions had anything to do with his one-time Fabian ardour.

It was owing to the manipulations of Marsh, once more, that his 'wanderings' were finally brought to an end. He had written to Andrew Gow, who was dealing with applications for commissions at Cambridge, when Marsh brought the news that a new unit was being created : it was to be called the Royal Naval Division under the command of a Major-General but administered by the Admiralty – that is, under Winston Churchill's control. It was to consist of men from the Royal Marines, the Naval Reserve, and unspecified others. Rupert jumped at the idea of this solution to his problems, as he had made up his mind that it was active service he wanted. Marsh wrote to him at Rugby that he was going to push the appointment of him and the ever-faithful Denis Browne 'for all I'm worth. I can make play with Winston having promised you an appointment.' He succeeded, and a few days later he was able to tell the two young men that there would be no fuss of interviews or forms to fill in, and they would be enrolled at once as Sub-Lieutenants in the RNVR, formally attached to HMS *Victory*. His destiny was now in the favouring hands of Winston Churchill.

Events moved swiftly at last. About a week later he lunched
with Marsh at the Admiralty, with Churchill as their host. He
wrote to Cathleen afterwards, partly to give her the news, but
even more to make some kind of apology for what he sensed
she must feel, in this so rapidly moving transformation scene,
as his lack of total love towards her:

'Winston was very cheerful at lunch, and said one thing
which is exciting, but a *dead* secret. You mustn't *breathe* it.
That is, that it's his game to hold the Northern ports – Dunkirk to Havre – at all costs. So if there's a raid on any of
them, at *any* moment, we shall be flung across to help the
French reservists. So we may go to Camp on Saturday, and
be under fire in France on Monday! I'm afraid the odds are
against it, though.

Your letter was a great comfort to me. I read it twice a
day.

Queer things are happening to me, and I'm frightened.
Oh, I've loved you a long time, child: but not in the complete way of love. I mean, there was something rooted out
of my heart by things that went before. I thought I couldn't
love wholly, again. I couldn't worship – I could see intellectually that some women were worshipful, perhaps. But I
couldn't find the flame of worship in me. I was unhappy.
Oh, God, I *knew* how glorious and noble your heart was. But,
I couldn't burn to it. I mean, I loved you with all there was
of me. But I was a cripple, incomplete.

Child, there's something growing in me. You have given
it me. I adore you. I love you in every other way: and I
worship the goodness in you. This has been growing in me.
I feel like a sick man who is whole again. It comes on me
more and more dazzlingly how infinitely you're the best
thing in my life: and that I might live a million years, and
never find anything so glorious as you, for me to adore and
pray to, nor anything so good in me as my love for you. . . .

Cathleen, if you *knew* how I adore you, and fight towards
you. I want to cut away the evil in me, and be wholly a thing
worthy of you. Be good to me, child. I sometimes think you
can make anything in the world of me. . . .'

For one thing, he was still worrying about Ka, who had
invited him to stay for a week-end. He said no, and tried to

write her a farewell letter again, reminding her of the strain
he believed they both had felt at their tea-shop meeting:

'And then, the thought of you – at least, if it's made vivid
by your presence – makes me deeply and bitterly ashamed
of myself. I don't know *why* – I mean, it's not that my mind
condemns me, especially, in any way. I only know that – inevitably or not – through me you have been greatly hurt, and
two or three years of your life – which can be so wonderful – have been changed and damaged. And I'm terribly
ashamed before you.

And there's just the general case of old wounds : that every-
body has a better chance, if they're given the best opportunities, to close and stay closed.

It's for these reasons, and only these, that I want not to
see you too frequently or too much. I was afraid that my
bad manners might have made it seem as if I thought you
boring perhaps.'

He ended his letter with a confession as if wrung out of him
by unhappiness at the deepest level :

'I don't seem to myself to do very much with my existence.
And I don't know of anything I very much want to do with
it. I think I find the world fairly good, on the whole, because
that handful of existences I know about and care for –
Dudley's and the rest – are, on the whole, happy and good.
But of them all yours has to be the one which seems to me
most important. Till I think you're complete, I shan't be
happy. When you're married and happy, I shall believe that
the world *is* good. Till then, I shall be conscious of – general
– failure. It's the one thing I hope for, in a confused world.
You see, you do seem *worth* so much. I shall probably see
you, incidentally, in the next few days or weeks, in con-
nexion with Dudley and Anne. Anyhow, I've tried to make
myself clear.'

Ever since he had fallen out of love with Ka, Rupert had been
given to outbursts of self-denunciation. At about this time he
wrote to Lady Eileen, with the instinct perhaps that something
like a love-affair was developing between them :

'So you puzzled your foolish but lovely head to know what

I meant by saying that I was "horrible". Well, I *am* horrible. And occasionally it comes over me that I am. And then I feel – for a few moments – wretched. As to *why* – or *how* – I'm horrible: it's harder to say. There are so many things. I'm not especially *fickle*-hearted. I'm not – *doch*, I *am* rather – hard-hearted. I usen't to be. I think one of the things which appals me is my extraordinary selfishness: which isn't quite the same as hardness of heart, though it helps. I mean, I just enjoy things as they come, & don't think or care how they affect other people. That, my gentle and adorable child, is why I felt uneasy & frightened about you, at first. I knew how often I did harm to people, through carelessness & selfishness.

And another thing is (this sounds like a catalogue of German atrocities) I'm really a wolf and a tiger and a goat. I am – how shall I put it – carried along on the tides of my body, rather helplessly. At intervals I realize this, and feel rather aghast.

Oh, it's all right if you don't *trust* me, my dear. *I* don't. Never trust me an inch.

Oh, I'm rather a horror. A vagabond, drifting from one imbecility to another. You don't know how pointless and undependable and rotten a thing you've got hold of.

Don't laugh. I know it's funny. But it's all true.'

Nevertheless he finished the letter on a different note:

'Well, child, if you're happy with me: that's something, isn't it? I'm certainly happy with you. We can have fun together, can't we? And supposing I go off & get blown to pieces – what fools we should feel if we hadn't had fun – if we'd foregone our opportunities – shouldn't we?

This is a stupid letter. I'm rather gray (I'm back in London, now, sooner than I thought, Sunday night): I've been bidding a modified farewell to my mother. Also, I'm tired.

It's so good being with you. You give me – much more than you know.

Be happy, child. Write about Tuesday. I love your variegated envelopes.

I kiss you good night. You'll get this in the morning. Never mind.

All Heaven be about you.'

It is scarcely possible to read these letters he wrote at this time, to Ka, to Cathleen Nesbitt, and to Lady Eileen, without being aware of his deep emotional confusion.

On Sunday 27 September he and Denis Browne were seen off by Marsh at Charing Cross. The 2nd Naval Brigade, which they were joining, consisted of five battalions – Drake, Howe, Hood, Nelson and Anson. They were posted to the Anson, Rupert as a Sub-Lieutenant in command of the 15th Platoon, D Company. They were encamped in Betteshanger Park, near the coast in Kent, on Lord Northbourne's estate.

Most of the men in Rupert's platoon were stokers, still in naval uniform, from Northumberland, the remoter parts of Scotland, and Ireland. He could scarcely understand what they said in their Celtic dialects, and told his friends that when asked their names they replied, totally unintelligibly, 'Mghchnghchchch'. But he liked them, and admired them, and told Lady Eileen that under other circumstances he might 'find incredible beauty in the washing place, with rows of naked, superb men, bathing in a September sun or in the Camp at night under a full moon, faint lights burning through the ghostly tents, and a distant bugler blowing *Lights Out*.' They boxed, they played football, they drilled; and waited.

Early on Sunday 4 October orders came to cross the Channel. The bugle sounded, there were cheers as they woke in their tents. They marched to Dover, behind a band which played current music-hall tunes: the favourite of Rupert's platoon was 'Hullo, who's your lady friend?' – and they roared it on the quay as they waited to embark. The news went round that their objective was Antwerp, the outer defences of which the Germans were already shelling. Two destroyers were waiting out at sea, and escorted them to Dunkirk. Twelve fatal hours were lost unloading equipment, and it was too late to hold the enemy while the Belgian forces retired towards Ghent. The senior officers told them that their train was almost certain to be shelled, and the likelihood was that they would man trenches briefly, only to be wiped out. With this cheerful prospect ahead of them, they spent the hours until their train left writing farewell letters home. The train was not attacked, and they reached Antwerp, where the Belgians cheered them wildly and shouted '*Vive les Anglais!*' as they marched through the streets.

They made their way to a place he called Vieux Dieu, which
was in a frenzied confusion of troops, guns, motor-cyclists and
staff cars forcing their way through, while the noise of battle
grew nearer and louder, explosions and detonations and
shrapnel bursting round aeroplanes high in the sky. The battalion was marched into the grounds of a nearby château,
where they spent the night. Rupert found a bedroom and tried
to sleep in the clatter of the guns and the whining of the shells
passing overhead, while the sailors dug their latrines among
the rose-beds, the frozen fountains and the glimmering statues.
At dawn they were ordered to move forward to relieve the
Belgians in their trenches round an antiquated strongpoint
called Fort 7. But the defence was crumbling under the weight
of the German attack; the station where their train was standing, and all their luggage and possessions – including MSS
Rupert was working on – went up in flames; the oil tanks at
Hoboken flooded the meadows with blazing petrol. The forts
were smashed by the German artillery, and the Council of
War in Antwerp decided they would have to withdraw. The
men of the Anson battalion started their march back to Saint-
Gilles, twenty-five miles behind them, where the troop-trains
waited, they were told, to evacuate them.

They marched back through Antwerp, deserted now except
for a few thousand beings who could not face, or would not
face, abandoning all. The flames of burning petrol licked across
the road, the smoke was suffocating and blinding, and created
a pall of darkness across the sky. The carcases of horses and
cattle, on the road and in the fields around them, sizzled as they
burned. They passed railway stations totally demolished, the
lines and signals ripped up, locomotives lying smashed across
the chaos. The scene, Rupert wrote later, was like Hell, 'a
Dantesque Hell, terrible'. But when they had crossed the
Scheldt by a pontoon bridge hastily flung across it, they came
across what he described as an even 'truer Hell', an experience
that was to change his whole attitude towards the war, and
wipe out the last traces of his sympathy for the Germans,
especially for the Prussians who were, as he saw it, leading the
rest of Germany into this colossal crime and horror. They
suddenly found themselves in the midst of the refugees:
thousands and thousands of them plodding westwards on the
road in an unending double line, the old men often weeping,

the women with the hard drawn faces of bitterness and total exhaustion, with what they had been able to rescue of their goods on barrows and carts and perambulators. The British contingent marched on in as good order as they could, with the refugees, Belgian troops, motor-buses and other transport swirling into an even thicker confusion around them. There were London buses in the midst of it, indicating with grotesque irrelevance that they were bound for Hammersmith or Fleet Street or theatre-land. 'After about a thousand years it was dawn.' They reached the troop-trains, and were carried on to Bruges. There they were able to eat and sleep briefly at last, out of reach of the guns. In the morning they moved on to Ostend, where they boarded a transport for Dover. Behind them, Antwerp had fallen.

The first thing that Rupert did on arrival in London, accompanied by Arthur 'Oc' Asquith, Violet's brother, who had been in the Anson battalion with him, was to hurry to the Admiralty. Dinner was over, and Marsh took them straight in to see Winston Churchill. They told him the story of their adventures, bit by bit, piecing it together as they went on, and of the fate of the expedition.

Churchill's enemies made much of the failure of the attempt to relieve Antwerp, but it has been forcibly argued that, though it had to withdraw so soon, it had prevented the Germans from gaining the Channel ports of Nieuport and Dunkirk, and from turning the northern flank of the Allies.

The next few months were a period of frustration and restlessness for Rupert. It was clearly sound policy for the Royal Naval Division to be kept by Churchill in reserve for the next opportunity to stage an armed assault from the sea; the Dardanelles adventure, the idea of destroying the efficacy of the Central Powers' Turkish ally and smashing a way through to join up with Russia from the south, and so providing a channel through which arms could be shipped to her hard-pressed armies and through which at the same time the rich grain harvests of the Ukraine could reach the Allies, had not yet been conceived. Rupert had suffered no harm in Belgium, except in shock of mind, though directly after return he developed one of the worst of his recurrent attacks of conjunctivitis. He went down to see his mother at Rugby, visited Cathleen whose touring play had reached Lowestoft, and mixed with his old friends again in London. One of the surprises he gave them was to turn up one day with Noel Olivier, by then twenty-two years old; unfortunately nothing is known of what led to their coming together again, nor what passed between them. It seems entirely improbable that either of them considered their engagement of four years earlier as anything but a dead letter. One would like to think that Noel herself, being as sensible as she had shown herself over the matter of the dedication to *Poems 1911*, encouraged Rupert not to feel unduly guilty about it.

In the middle of October he rejoined his unit at Betteshanger. He had started to write his war sonnets, and worked on them in the intervals of his military duties. The new mood which they embodied also showed itself in his changed attitude towards those of his friends and acquaintances who were not as dedicated as he had now become to the winning of the war. He made the astonishing declaration – astonishing from the sceptical atheist of Cambridge days and the author of *An Unusual Young Man* – in a letter to Cathleen that the central purpose of his life, 'the aim and end of it, now, the thing God wants of me, is to get good at beating Germans. That's sure.' His former Bloomsbury friends were, of course, beyond the pale; but even when E. J. Dent wrote asking him whether he would contribute to a fund the aim of which was to help a consumptive friend to spend the winter in Los Angeles, he replied, with more than a touch of the convert's priggishness, that he felt 'it's not a time to be wintering in Los Angeles', and that 'if anyone *has* any spare money, he should be trying to assist with it some of the outcast Belgian widows and children'. He gave Dent a lecture on how to behave even if one was afflicted by a dangerous illness: 'I know a girl who is consumptive. Her doctor said she'd probably die if she didn't spend this winter in a sanitorium. She's doing Belgian refugee organization and clothing in London: and is going to stay at it.'

The lurking Puritan in his make-up was asserting itself ever more strongly. He began to feel that women should not appear on the stage at all, and wrote to Cathleen: 'If you were a man there'd be no excuse for you to go on acting. You'd be despicable', clearly hinting that whatever her sex he didn't like her being on the stage at this particular time. A curiously reactionary attitude for the enthusiastic co-founder of the Marlowe Society.

He wrote to his American friend Russell Loines to give him a picture of how he thought patriotic Englishmen should behave – and were behaving:

> 'It's astonishing to see how the "intellectuals" have taken on new jobs (no, not astonishing: but impressive). Masefield drills hard in Hampstead and told me with some pride, a month ago, that he was a Corporal and *thought* he was going to be promoted to Sergeant soon. Cornford is no longer the best Greek scholar in Cambridge. He recalled that he was a very good shot in his youth, and is a Sergeant-Instructor of Musketry. I'm here. My brother is a 2nd Lieutenant in the Post Office Rifles. He was one of three great friends at King's. The second is Intelligence Officer on H.M.S. *Vengeance*, Channel Patrol. The third is buried near Cambrai. Gilbert Murray and Walter Raleigh rise at six every day to line hedgerows in the dark and "advance in rushes" across the Oxford meadows. Among the other officers in this Division are two young Asquiths, an Australian professional pianist who twice won the Diamond Sculls, a New Zealander who was fighting in Mexico and walked three hundred miles to the coast to get a boat when he heard of the war, a friend of mine Denis Browne – Cambridge – who is one of the best young English musicians and an extremely brilliant critic, a youth lately through Eton and Balliol who is the most brilliant man they've had in Oxford for years, a young and very charming American John Bigelow Dodge who turned up to fight "for the right" – I could extend the list. It's all a terrible thing. And yet, in its details, it's great fun. . . .'

By the time he wrote this letter he had been transferred from the Anson battalion to the Hood, which was encamped near Blandford in Dorset: a great improvement because the Commanding Officer of the Anson had proved extremely unpopular, and because very soon, as he indicated to Russell Loines, he was joined by Denis Browne, Arthur 'Oc' Asquith, and 'the most brilliant man they've had in Oxford for years', Patrick Shaw-Stewart, who was already known to him as an occasional visitor to Marsh's Raymond Buildings flat, and was to become a close friend in this last phase of his life. Shaw-

Stewart belonged to that remarkable Balliol circle of young men, Etonians all, that included Charles Lister, son of Lord Ribblesdale, and Julian and Billy Grenfell. Shaw-Stewart was perhaps the most striking in looks, tall, red-headed, blue-eyed and freckled, with an astonishingly long but not unattractive nose. The Commanding Officer of his company was Bernard Freyberg, a New Zealander who was to prove himself an outstandingly brave and brilliant soldier, and had a special bond with Rupert in the fact that he knew the South Seas well.

At Blandford the usual naval pretence of being on board ship was kept up: expeditions to the town were called 'going ashore', and a ship's bell sounded the watches. Rupert had a room in a wooden hut which he shared with seven other officers, and bombarded his mother and the practical Ka Cox with urgent requests for furnishings, for games to keep the sailors happy and festive food to enliven their Christmas. They were, it seems, fed up with being incarcerated ashore when they had hoped to be on a real ship, and the problem was to keep them from getting drunk all the time.

Rupert's illnesses continued to pursue him. Violet Asquith arrived one day before Christmas to find her brother feeling very sorry for himself and Rupert almost equally low, and managed to take them off to Lady Wimborne's house at Canford to recuperate. The ministering hands of his new friends were constantly around him. During his leave, which started on 30 December, Violet invited him to spend a couple of nights at Walmer Castle, and directly afterwards he made a dash for London and lunched at the Admiralty with the Churchills and the Prime Minister, together with Denis Browne. The pace was too much for him. By the beginning of February 1915 he had contracted such a severe chill that he was moved, at Violet's insistence, to No. 10 Downing Street, where he stayed for nine days and was visited by Goldie Lowes Dickinson and Henry James. Once more recovered, he lunched again at the Admiralty with Marsh, and afterwards, when Marsh had gone back to his work, had a long tête-à-tête with Churchill. We do not know whether during that discussion the First Lord hinted at the scheme that was at last maturing, hastened by the pleas of the Russians – the urgent request for help from the Grand Duke Nicholas arrived on 2 January – for the Dardanelles expedition; but it was not long before he arrived at Blandford for an official inspection of his Royal Naval Division, certain prelude to a move. Three days later Colonel Quilter, their Commanding Officer, gathered his officers around him and told them of the plan that had now become official. They were all tremendously excited at the prospect of being in action at last, and as part of an expedition that had such exotic implications. Rupert wrote to his mother, swearing her to secrecy: 'We are going to be part of a landing force to help the fleet break through the Hellespont and the Bosphorus and take Constantinople, and open up the Black Sea.' And to his friend Dudley Ward he exclaimed: 'Figure me celebrating the first Holy Mass in St Sophia since 1453!' He reckoned that they would take about a fortnight on the journey, be fighting for anything up to six weeks, and be back in May. 'I've never been quite so happy in my life, I think,' he wrote to Violet, assuming that as the Prime Minister's daughter she was in the know. He dreamed of a battle with the Turks on the plains of Troy. 'O Violet, it's too wonderful for belief. I had not imagined Fate could be so benign.'

On the 24th a group of friends from London came down to Blandford for the King's visit the next day. They included Marsh, Mrs Churchill, Violet Asquith and Lady Gwendolen Churchill. Early on the morning of the 25th Rupert breakfasted alone with Marsh, and then after the march-past, saw him driving alone up to London and turn and wave to him.

On the evening of the 27th the battalion marched to Shillingstone, where they entrained for Avonmouth Docks.

Violet Asquith stayed behind at Blandford to be with her brother, and then, armed with a special pass, followed the battalion to Avonmouth to see the departure. On Sunday 28 February she wrote in her diary:

'I made my way past many ships before I reached the *Grantully Castle*. I watched and waited for a Hood cap and then asked for Oc. He was on board shaving. . . . Denis Browne came and took charge of me and said he would go for Oc. Rupert appeared. He had "failli", had to stay on board but had just managed to exchange his watch with Kelly and was free till 4. Oc joined us and we went off to an hotel recommended by Edwin Montagu, surrounded by sham rockeries.

It was not *quite* all our fancy had pictured but not too bad
for all that. They seemed quite happy about their food which
was the main thing. There was a long discussion about what
their last drink should be and Burgundy was finally decided
on. After luncheon Rupert's chief desire was, as usual, to
get as warm as possible and we coiled ourselves almost *in*
the fireplace till it was time to go and get a prescription
made up for Patrick's throat – which was more than usually
poisoned that day. Being Sunday the chemist had to be
knocked up with some difficulty. Rupert and I sat talking
outside in the car while we waited and he showed me a
lovely little new poem beginning "When colour is gone
home into the eyes". He said in his usual, intensely quiet
modest-eyed way, "I think the first line perfectly divine."

We went back to the ship, dear Charles [Lister] passing
us on the way and looking as mad as twenty hatters and as
gay. Quilter in a taxi we easily outstripped. On arrival at
the Quay we found to our dismay that the ship had moved
and was lying in the mouth of the harbour! We felt safe
however with the C.O. behind us. I saw and spoke to him
for a moment, also George Peel, then I went on board the
Transport with them. It was a not-bad Union Castle boat
and they were only two in a cabin. I went in to see poor
Patrick who was lying in his bunk among cough mixtures and
bandages looking as green as grass and very septic. I lingered
on with Oc and Rupert with a terrible pre-operation feeling.
The suspended knife seemed just above us all. Then the dull
muffled siren booms began, charged with finality, and we
knew that it was falling. Rupert walked with me along the
narrow crowded decks, down the plank stairs. I said good-bye
to him. I saw in his eyes that he felt sure we should never
see each other again.

Oc took me over the gangway and we talked for a few
moments feverishly – "I shall come back," he said. "I may
be wounded but I shall come back." Another imperious hoot
and he had to hurry back. The gangway was raised and the
ship moved slowly out, the Hood trumpeters playing a salute
on their silver trumpets as it passed the mouth of the harbour.
The decks were densely crowded with young, splendid
figures, happy, resolute and confident – and the thought of the

Athenian expedition against Syracuse flashed irresistibly through my mind. . . .'

By then Rupert had completed all five of his war sonnets, and had sent them off to *New Numbers*.

13

The War Sonnets

The main work on the five war sonnets appears to have been done between the Antwerp expedition and the departure for the Dardanelles; much of it probably in camp at Blandford, or in the intervals of sick leave at Lady Wimborne's house at Canford. In any case, he mentions in a letter to Eileen Wellesley that he was writing the last, and most famous sonnet, 'If I should die', late at night after the Christmas celebrations in camp and after he managed to get the last of the drunken stokers back to their bunks. He may have polished them during his New Year leave at Rugby. He had sent them off to *New Numbers* before 13 January 1915, the day on which Wilfred Gibson acknowledged them.

It is difficult to say what Rupert Brooke's reputation as a poet would have been if he had not written these sonnets at that particular moment in the war. He would, one cannot help thinking, have been seen as one of the most gifted verse-writers of his generation, but not more outstanding than such contempories as W. H. Davies, Walter de la Mare and Lascelles Abercrombie. It was the war sonnets that changed him into the almost sacred, supreme poet-figure of his generation, the mellifluous mouthpiece of the sentiments that had before been half incoherently felt by all those English people who were struggling to make sense of the war into which they had so suddenly been plunged, and who clung to the hope that the trials and sufferings, still only mistily revealed, that lay before them could be considered as part of a crusade of right against wrong, as a testing ground of courage and belief in their own country and its cause.

At the same time it is possible that with a subsequent generation who saw the noble sentiments as glib idealism and unrealistic day-dreaming, his name might not have fallen into the disrepute that has lasted until today; a generation whose fathers and elder brothers had lived through the senseless horrors of the Flanders trenches, and who found in the poetry of Siegfried Sassoon, Wilfred Owen and Isaac Rosenberg the true response to modern warfare at its most futile and morally degrading. No thoughtful and sensitive young man could imaginably have gone into the fighting of the Second World War with the lines of Brooke's sonnets *The Dead* and *Peace* echoing in his mind to inspire his vision and steel his purpose. If, however, those sonnets had not been written, such young men might still have delighted in the lyrical freshness of *Tiare Tahiti*, the light-hearted nostalgia of *Grantchester*, and the debunking wit and technical skill of his remodelled fish poem, *Heaven*; and a number of others where the sentiment is not forced and the language keeps rhetoric under a more caustic intellectual control. That he had seen how important such discipline was is shown by his whole-hearted admiration for the poetry of John Donne.

I have already spoken admiringly of *Heaven*, and I feel that at this point I should quote it in full :

> Fish (fly-replete, in depth of June,
> Dawdling away their wat'ry noon)
> Ponder deep wisdom, dark or clear,
> Each secret fishy hope or fear.
> Fish say, they have their Stream and Pond;
> But is there anything Beyond?
> This life cannot be All, they swear,
> For how unpleasant, if it were!
> One may not doubt that, somehow, Good
> Shall come of Water and of Mud;
> And, sure, the reverent eye must see
> A Purpose in Liquidity.
> We darkly know, by Faith we cry,
> The future is not Wholly Dry.
> Mud unto mud! – Death eddies near –
> Not here the appointed End, not here !
> But somewhere, beyond Space and Time,
> Is wetter water, slimier slime !
> And there (they trust) there swimmeth One

Who swam ere rivers were begun,
Immense, of fishy form and mind,
Squamous, omnipotent, and kind;
And under that Almighty Fin,
The littlest fish may enter in.
Oh! never fly conceals a hook,
Fish say, in the Eternal Brook,
But more than mundane weeds are there,
And mud, celestially fair;
Fat caterpillars drift around,
And Paradisal grubs are found;
Unfading moths, immortal flies,
And the worm that never dies.
And in that Heaven of all this wish,
There shall be no more land, say fish.

Brooke's poetry gives the impression of great ease and fluency; but we know from a number of witnesses, intimate friends who were with him when he was at work, and fellow writers, that he worked with great care, often re-wrote a number of times, and would leave gaps in his lines until he could find what he judged to be the exactly right word or phrase.

The chief weakness of his poetry – and it is a weakness markedly in contrast to the mastery in this particular sphere shown by Donne and by his almost equally admired Webster – was a preference for vague grandiloquence and high-sounding generalities in preference to the concrete word and the freshly illuminating image, the poetical cliché instead of the original imaginative discovery. It may be partly due to a lingering fondness for the affected romanticism of the nineties he had felt in his youthful phase; it continued to slip into his more mature poetry all too often when his mind was not working at top pressure.

Phrases such as 'in wise majestic melancholy train', 'some low sweet alley between wind and wind', 'dark scents whisper', 'the grey tumult of these after-years', 'song's nobility and wisdom holy', 'the heart of bravery swift and clean', which have a fine exalted ring but when examined mean nothing precise at all, from time to time pad out his verses throughout his adult career and not merely his beginnings when he was searching for a style; in fact they become his style as soon as he forgets his wit and light-heartedness and abandons those realistic touches that so shocked the critics of his first book. With what relief, then, one comes across the precise and vivid images with which in *The Great Lover* he enumerates the concrete things that evoke his love in recollection : 'wet roofs, beneath the lamplight', 'the rough male kiss of blankets', 'the good smell of old clothes', 'brown horse-chestnuts, glossy new'; though even in this attractive and original, though imperfect, poem he cannot resist the glib poetical rhetoric of phrases such as 'the inenarrable godhead of delight' and 'out on the wind of Time, shining and streaming'.

The weakness of the war sonnets lies not merely in their even more fulsome use of such insubstantial rhetoric, but in the fundamental shallowness and inadequacy of the sentiments expressed in relation to the grimness of the challenge which faced the young men on the German as well as the British side. Two years after Rupert Brooke's death the nature of the beast was fully apparent to the armies engaged in the fighting, if not to the civilians in the comparative safety of Britain; but one should after all remember that before he left on the Dardanelles expedition Rupert had had a glimpse, which shocked and deeply affected his outlook, of the reality of modern mechanized slaughter and destruction.

The vague high-sounding generalities appear so profusely in the sonnets that it would be tedious to list them all. Worst of all, perhaps, in this respect is the second sonnet, *Safety*. The poet, addressing his beloved, enumerates the phenomena, 'all things undying', which make them feel 'safe' :

> The winds, and morning, tears of men and mirth
> The deep night, and birds singing, and clouds flying,
> And sleep, and freedom, and the autumnal earth.

Every image in these lines is obvious and of the most general kind, and contributes nothing concrete to the idea, or makes any imaginative discovery that can be called in any way original : it is little more than a lulling incantation of clichés. The same process is almost disastrously at work in the fourth sonnet, called *The Dead* like the third, in which we are bidden to lament the death of the young soldiers because their hearts were

Washed marvellously with sorrow, swift to mirth.
The years had given them kindness. Dawn was theirs,
And sunset, and the colours of the earth.
These had seen movement, and heard music. . . .

And when in their death they are compared with the effect of
frost on 'waves that dance / And wandering loveliness' (whatever that last phrase may mean), we are told that they leave 'a
white

> Unbroken glory, a gathered radiance,
> A width, a shining peace, under the night',

one can only register astonishment that Brooke, who could be
so precise when he liked, can crowd so many nouns denoting
vaguely emotive general concepts, 'unbroken glory', 'gathered
radiance', 'shining peace' into two lines.

The two most quoted and probably most popular sonnets –
certainly most popular at the time – are the first, *Peace*, and
the fifth, *The Soldier*. The first, *Peace*, is the sonnet that most
successors of a younger generation, and probably most soldiers
who saw more of the war than Rupert ever saw, have jibbed
at as shallowy sentimental and unrealistic. What soldier, who
had experienced the meaningless horror and foulness of the
Western Front stalemate in 1916 and 1917, could think of it
as a place to greet 'as swimmers into cleanness leaping' or as
a welcome relief 'from a world grown old and cold and weary'?
These are the sentiments of one who at least had had no opportunity to face the reality of twentieth-century warfare – killing
and maiming and being killed and maimed in the most appalling
ways by the most devilish devices of terror. To say that is not
to deny admiration for those, in both wars, who were aware
of what they were facing and chose it out of determination to
defend what they believed was worth defending – and Rupert
Brooke might well have been one of those if he had lived and
been active as a soldier in 1917; nor to deny that such an attitude
as finds expression in *Peace* was common to many poets, on
both sides of the frontiers, in the curious excitement and
hysteria that the outbreak of war in 1914 aroused.

What is peculiarly disturbing about *Peace* is that it gives
sudden and violent expression to Rupert's always latent puritanism. The soldiers are awakened 'from sleeping' and are
leaping 'into cleanness' in getting away from their everyday

pursuits (though *The Dead* seems to express an entirely opposite point of view); fighting redeems a world 'grown old and cold and weary' even though it involves killing and destruction and waste; the whole of Rupert's past life is characterized as

> The sick hearts that honour could not move,
> And half-men, and their dirty songs and dreary,
> And all the little emptiness of love.

Who are these 'half-men' and 'sick hearts' unmoved by honour? What poet was singing 'dirty songs and dreary'? Were his passionate and unhappy involvements with Ka Cox and his new, joyful love for Cathleen Nesbitt to be brushed aside as 'all the little emptiness of love'? Or was he thinking again, obsessively, of the emotional shocks he endured at Lulworth in the New Year of 1912, with Lytton Strachey and other denizens of Bloomsbury as the 'sick hearts' and 'half-men' who wounded him so mysteriously? And if so, why did they now become symbols of all that had made up civilian existence before the war, as if civilized peaceful living itself was only worth throwing away *in toto*?

The Soldier is as eloquent and skilful a piece of verse-making as anything Rupert ever produced, with its repeated plangent harping on the word 'England' and all the historic and patriotic overtones it evoked. The movement of the argument and the tone are both flawless, and one can easily see how in the anxious, emotional mood of the early months of the war it could bring tears to any sensitive eye. And yet, looked at dispassionately today, it is difficult not to feel that it is riddled with sentimentality and narcissistic fantasy, whatever he may have meant in imagining himself 'a pulse in the eternal mind' purified of all unworthy thought and feeling. Even at the time, while the guns were still thundering, there were not a few, and among them his intellectual peers, who questioned his attitudinizing. One of these, his fellow poet Charles Sorley, eight years younger, wrote to a friend when he heard of Rupert's death that he found the sonnet sequence over-praised:

> 'He is far too obsessed with his own sacrifice, regarding the going to war of himself (and others) as a highly intense, remarkable and sacrificial exploit, whereas it is merely the conduct demanded of him (and others) by the turn of cir-

cumstances, where non-compliance with this demand would have made life intolerable. It was not that "they" gave up anything of that list in one sonnet: but that the essence of these things had been endangered by circumstances over which he had no control, and he must fight to recapture them. He has clothed his attitude in fine words: but he has taken the sentimental attitude.'

Part Three

14
End in the Aegean

On the evening of 11 March the expedition, with the Royal Naval Division aboard the *Grantully Castle*, reached Lemnos, which the Greek Government had granted the Allies as a base, though it refused to come into the War. Lemnos had been chosen as the most suitable Greek island, with its excellent deep-water anchorage of Mudros Bay, for the assault on the Dardanelles. The harbour was already filling up with Allied warships, including one Russian battleship. The troops from the *Grantully Castle* spent a week exploring the island, Rupert imagining that in certain lights he could see as far as Olympus and Parnassus. They were kept in complete darkness about plans: the Turks could hardly not have been aware of the gathering of Allied forces so close to their shores. There had been a successful naval bombardment of the forts in February, but owing to divided counsels in London and the general shilly-shallying that took place between the naval, military and political leaders, it could not be followed up at the time by a landing of troops.

On 10 March, from on board the *Grantully Castle*, he wrote to Ka Cox:

'I suppose you're the best I can do in the way of a widow. I'm telling the Ranee that after she's dead, you're to have my papers. They *may* want to write a biography! How am I to know if I shant be eminent? And take any MSS you want. Say what you like to the Ranee. But you'd better not tell her much. Let her be. Let her think we might have married. Perhaps it's true.

My dear, my dear, you did me wrong: but I have done you very great wrong. Every day I see it greater.

You were the best thing I found in life. If I have memory, I shall remember. You know what I want for you. I hope you will be happy, and marry and have children.

It's a good thing I die. Goodbye, child. Rupert.'

The day before he had written to Marsh to say that he was to be his literary executor, but his mother was to have the MSS till she died. There was an ambiguity about the instructions which was to cause much trouble later.

On 18 March orders came at last to prepare for a landing, and a few thousand of them sailed for the Straits through the night. In the early morning, parading on the ship's deck, they could see land, silent, not a soul, not a soldier in sight. Then, after some hours of silent waiting, the anti-climax came: they were ordered back to Lemnos. They were told they had taken part in a feint attack; what they did not know was that there had been another heavy bombardment of the coastal defences on the 18th in preparation for a breakthrough, but the warships found the waters thickly mined and losses had been severe. The admiral in charge appears to have lost his nerve, and refused to carry the plan through; though by that delay the Allies lost the chance of action before the Peninsula was heavily and cunningly reinforced by the Turks, aided by the Germans.

Rupert had clearly intended his letter of the 10th to be his final word to Ka, but meanwhile a letter from her crossed his, and in his pleasure he wrote her an account of the 'feint attack'.

'The darkness on the sea was full of scattered flashing lights, hinting at our fellow-transports and the rest. Slowly the day became wan and green and the sea opal. Everyone's face looked drawn and ghastly. If we landed, my company was to be the first to land. . . . We made out that we were only a mile or two from a dim shore. I was seized with an agony of remorse that I hadn't taught my platoon a thousand things more energetically and competently. The light grew. The shore looked to be crammed with Fate, and most ominously silent. One man thought he saw a camel through his glasses. . . .'

A few days later they again left Lemnos, but this time for

Port Said. Their camp was dismal, but the officers were being given leave for Cairo, three every forty-eight hours. Rupert left with Shaw-Stewart, and they stayed at Shepheard's Hotel. The next morning but one, back in camp, Shaw-Stewart began to feel ill, and developed an attack of dysentery: he felt certain he had a touch of sunstroke. He drove to the Casino Palace Hotel and took a room. Rupert was also beginning to feel ill. He lay on the camp-bed outside the tent, in order to be cooler in the light sea-breezes. While he lay there he was unexpectedly visited by Sir Ian Hamilton, the Commander-in-Chief, who was already anxious about him. He offered him a staff appointment at HQ on the *Queen Elizabeth*. Rupert refused. In the early afternoon, already in high fever, he took a cab to Shaw-Stewart's hotel and arranged to have a bed put up in the same room. Like Shaw-Stewart, he was now suffering from violent dysentery. Also he began to be troubled by a sore on the side of his upper lip, which swelled and throbbed. Later it was diagnosed as (most probably) a mosquito bite. It subsided, or appeared to subside. His condition slowly improved, and a few days later he and Shaw-Stewart sailed with their contingent back to Lemnos. Rupert stayed in bed most of the time, but had started light duties by the time they reached the island in the *Grantully Castle*.

On the first day at sea he wrote in his journal, which contained only one other entry besides this, in a seemingly dream-like state:

'There are moments – there have been several, especially in the Aegean – when, through some beauty of sky and air and earth, and some harmony with the mind, peace is complete and completely satisfying. One is at rest from the world, and with it, entirely content, drinking to the full of the placidity of the loveliness. Every second seems divine and sufficient. And there are men and women who seem to do what one so terribly can't, and so terribly at these moments, *aches* to do – store up reservoirs of this calm and content, fill and seal great jars or pitchers during these half-hours, and draw on them at later moments, when the source isn't there, but the need is very great. I wish there were more people of that character about on this expedition. . . .'

When they reached Mudras Bay they found it so full of shipping that they were ordered to turn round and sail south to the island of Skyros, where they found anchorage in Trebukis Bay. 'Oc' Asquith wrote a vivid description of the island to his sister Violet. 'It is like one great rock-garden of white and pink marble, with small red poppies and every kind of wildflower; in the gorges ilex, dwarf holly and occasional groups of olives – and everywhere the smell of thyme (or is it sage? or wild mint?). Our men kill adders to have fun with great tortoises. The water near the shore where the bottom is white marble is more beautifully green and blue than I have ever seen it anywhere.' The island was famous in legend: Theseus was said to have been murdered there by Lycomedus; and Achilles concealed in the house of Lycomedus' daughters; while, according to Homer, Neoptolemus, Achilles' son, was enticed thence to Troy by Ulysses. They used these classical references in their letters home to elude the censor in indicating where they were.

On the 20th there was a Divisional Field Day, in which Rupert took part. It was during their manoeuvres that Denis Browne accompanied Rupert, Charles Lister and Shaw-Stewart to an olive grove he had discovered, consisting of about a dozen trees, a place of exceptional beauty, above a dry river bed. They rested there. Rupert found the place full of a strange magic and peace. His friends remembered his pleasure in it, and three days later chose it as his last resting place.

Before the Field Day he had received a letter from Marsh telling him of the extraordinary event on Easter Sunday, when the Dean of St Paul's, Dean Inge, had preached on a text from Isaiah: 'The dead shall live, my dead bodies shall arise. Awake and sing, ye that dwell in the dust.' He told the congregation (*The Times* reported) that he had just read a poem on this subject by 'a young writer who would, he ventured to think, take rank with our great poets.' He proceeded to read 'If I should die' from the pulpit, and commented that 'the enthusiasm of a pure and elevated patriotism had never found a nobler expression. And yet it fell somewhat short of Isaiah's vision and still more of the Christian hope' – maintaining that a true Christian would be unable to think of a brave man's soul only finding immortality as 'a pulse in the eternal mind'.

Rupert seemed particularly tired after the Field Day, and

was very silent at the dinner party he and his friends were giving to a few friends from the *Franconia*. They were drinking hock, and as soon as the meal was over Rupert told Shaw-Stewart that he believed the wine was making his lip swell again. He made his excuses, and went straight to bed.

Denis Browne wrote a long letter to Marsh after everything was over. I will let him take up the story: his account cannot be improved:

'Next morning he stayed in bed, feeling seedy I heard. Somehow I did not see him until after dinner that night, when I looked in to ask how he was & to show him *The Times* cutting of Inge's sermon with the quotation of his sonnet. He said he felt very bad & didn't want the light on. He then said he had seen the cutting (did you send it?) & was sorry Inge didn't think he was as good as Isaiah. He complained of a swelling on the left side of his upper lip. He was evidently not up to very much, & I left him.

Next morning (Thursday) he was worse. The Battn. surgeon (McCracken) was not anxious about his lip, but was worried because he had pain in his chest & back. I looked in three times during the day, but he was dozing and I didn't like to disturb him. At midday McCracken got really anxious & sent for the A.D.M.S. Gaskell, the D.A.D.M.S. Casement, & the Brigade S.M.O. Schlesinger (whom I recognized as a Guy's man). They came over about 3 and consulted with McCracken & Goodall (the ship's surgeon & a good bacteriologist), & the conclusion they arrived at was that he had practically no chance of getting over it: the diagnosis was acute blood-poisoning. They proposed operating by making an incision in an abscess which had formed on the left side of the neck & was pumping the infected blood from his lip all over the body. But before they could do this, we had the idea of getting him on to a hospital ship. There was a French hospital ship, the *Duguay-Trouin*, in Skyros, and we asked them to take him in, as anything would have been better than the stuffy cabin he was in, and there were no proper facilities on the *Grantully Castle* for nursing him. In less than half an hour we had carried him down into a pinnace and taken him straight aboard the *Duguay-Trouin*.

They put him in the best cabin, one of two set back-to-back on the sun deck aft, on the highest part of the ship. She was originally a naval school at Brest, built in 1878, & was converted in 24 hours into a hospital: everything was very roomy and comfortable, if old-fashioned; but they had every modern appliance & the surgeons did everything they possibly could. He was practically the only patient on the ship & the chief surgeon gave up his whole time to the case, & I believe hardly left him at all. Whether they made the incision in his neck on Thursday night I don't know. Schlesinger said they would probably "irrigate" the place with antiseptic. Oc and I left him about 6 when we could do nothing more & went to the *Franconia*, where we sent a wireless message to Admiralty & also one to the G.O.C. in C. at Lemnos. We had hoped that he might be able to send either the *Sudan* or the *Cecilia* off to Skyros, or, failing that, to send a couple of sisters from the *Cecilia* in a destroyer. But that would have been no use as Gaskell said it would be impossible to move him again on to another ship: and as a matter of fact all the G.O.C. did was (I believe) to send a message to ask how he was.

Next morning Oc & I went over in a steam pinnace soon after breakfast to see what we could do: and found him very much weaker, but not quite so bad as Schlesinger expected. I stayed on board till 2.30, but there was nothing to be done as he was quite unconscious & they were busy trying all the devices they could think of to do him good & give him ease. Not that he was suffering, for he was barely conscious all Thursday (he just said "Hallo" when I went to lift him out into the pinnace) & on Friday he was not conscious at all up to the very last & felt no pain whatever. At 2 o'clock the head surgeon told me he was sinking & I went off to the *Franconia* for the Chaplain for his mother's sake. The chaplain (Failes by name) came back with me & saw him, but he was unconscious so after saying a few prayers he went away. Oc had arrived at 2.30 & I brought Schlesinger from the *Royal George*. He confirmed the change & told me it was simply a matter of hours. Oc then went off to see about preliminary arrangements and I sat with Rupert. At 4 o'clock he became weaker and at 4.46 he died.

We had orders to sail next morning at 6 for Gallipoli: and the French ship was off at the same moment for Asia Minor. So Oc and I had to decide at once what to do.

We buried him the same evening in the olive grove I mentioned before – one of the loveliest places on this earth, with grey-green olives round him, one weeping above his head: the ground covered with flowering sage, bluish grey & smelling more delicious than any other flower I know. The path up to it from the sea is narrow & difficult and very stony: it runs by the bed of a dried-up torrent. He was carried up from the boat by his A Company petty officers, led by his platoon-sergeant Saunders: and it was with enormous difficulty that they got the coffin up the narrow way. The journey of a mile took two hours. It was not till 11 that I saw them coming (I had gone up to choose the place & with Freyberg & Charles Lister I turned the sods of his grave: we had some of his platoon to dig). First came one of his men carrying a great white wooden cross with his name painted on it in black: then the firing party, commanded by Patrick [Shaw-Stewart]; & then the coffin followed by our officers, General Paris, Saunders & one or two others of the Brigade Staff. The Commodore could not be there, nor was Maxwell. Think of it under a clouded moon, with the three mountains around & behind us, and those divine scents everywhere. We lined his grave with all the flowers we could find & Quilter set a wreath of olive on the coffin. The funeral service was very simply said by the Chaplain and after the Last Post the little lamp-lit procession went once again down the narrow path to the sea.

Freyberg, Oc, I, Charles and Cleg [Kelly] stayed behind & covered the grass with great pieces of white marble which were lying everywhere about. Of the cross at his head you know: it was the large one that headed the procession. On the back of it our Greek interpreter, a man picked up by Oc at Lemnos, wrote in pencil [translation]:

> Here lies
> The servant of God
> Sub-Lieutenant in the
> English Navy

Who died for
The deliverance of
Constantinople from
The Turks.

It was quite spontaneous, and, don't you think, apt. At his feet was a wooden cross sent by his platoon.

We could not see the grave again as we sailed from Skyros the next morning at 6.

These are some of the bare facts: forgive me for telling them so confusedly & badly. I have had so many interruptions – all day we have been waiting for orders to land on Gallipoli. . . .'

Later, Denis Browne wrote again to Marsh, when they were already under fire, lying within 6,000 yards of land, and said of Colonel Freyberg: 'he has been wonderful the last few days. He loved and understood Rupert intuitively in spite of the differences in their temperaments; and last night, when we were making the grave, he was as gentle as a woman, and as strong as a giant.' A final letter followed at the beginning of June, written as if he were already dead – by then the casualties had mounted up at an appalling rate. 'I've gone now too; not too badly I hope. I'm luckier than Rupert, because I've fought. But there's no one to bury me as I buried him, so perhaps he's better off in the long run.' He was killed in trench fighting on 7 June: his death was almost as great a grief to Marsh as Rupert's had been.

On 9 March, while they were at sea, Rupert had written to Marsh, confirming that he wanted him to be his literary executor, but that his actual papers and MSS should be kept by his mother until her death. To Ka he wrote the letter I have already quoted. He had arranged that Wilfred Gibson and Lascelles Abercrombie and Walter de la Mare were to share his royalties – a bequest that was to be of a richness he could not have conceived – 'to help them write good stuff, instead of me.'

In Rupert's notebook, which they transcribed during the night before they left, his friends found a moving fragment of poetry which, echoing the entry in his journal, seemed strangely apt to the fate of its author:

... He wears
The ungathered blossom of quiet; stiller he
Than a deep well at noon, or lovers met;
Than sleep, or the heart after wrath. He is
The silence following great words of peace.

15

Aftermath and Canonization

The process of canonizing Rupert Brooke, and turning him into the supreme symbol of the generation of young men who were being sacrificed in the war, had, as we have seen, begun before his death with the sermon on Easter Sunday by the Dean of St Paul's, and his reading from the pulpit of the sonnet beginning 'If I should die, think only this of me.' In no time at all the issue of *New Numbers* which had printed the sonnets was sold out. It could not be reprinted, as there was no more paper available under wartime restrictions, and, as I have said, the little business closed down for good. Rupert himself was dead less than three weeks later, but he had been well and truly launched on his glittering, posthumous river of fame.

If one wishes to be cynical, one can say that Rupert's death, occurring as it did so soon after his 1914 sonnets had become public property, was a god-send for the politicians and generals who used him – perhaps without fully realizing what they were doing – to create a legendary inspiration for the national cause, a mouthpiece for patriotic sentiments that demanded simple, exalted expression beyond the range of the ranting of the newspapers and the tub-thumping demagogues. The war was not going well; it was turning out to be a far greater ordeal than anyone in high places had imagined possible when it was declared; and the full disaster of the Dardanelles campaign was to become glaringly apparent only a few weeks later.

On 26 April, three days after the death, a short unsigned obituary (in fact written by Marsh), fond but dignified, was printed in *The Times*. It ended : 'He died before he had fulfilled his own hopes or ours; but either we believe in waste altogether or not at all. And if any seeming waste is not waste, there is none in a young life full of promise and joyfully laid down.'

This was eclipsed, however, by a long, high-flown commemoration over the initials of the First Lord of the Admiralty. It must be quoted in full, because of its significance in the building up of the Brooke legend, even though it contains phrases that can hardly fail to provoke revulsion today :

'Rupert Brooke is dead. A telegram from the Admiralty at Lemnos tells us that this life has closed at the moment when it seemed to have reached its springtime. A voice had become audible, a note had been struck, more true, more thrilling, more able to do justice to the nobility of our youth in arms engaged in this present war, than any other – more able to express their thoughts of self-surrender, and with a power to carry comfort to those who watched them so intently from afar. The voice has been swiftly stilled. Only the echoes and the memory remain; but they will linger.

During the last few months of his life, months of preparation in gallant comradeship and open air, the poet-soldier told with all the simple force of genius the sorrow of youth about to die, and the sure triumphant consolations of a sincere and valiant spirit. He expected to die; he was willing to die for the dear England whose beauty and majesty he knew; and he advanced towards the brink in perfect serenity, with absolute conviction of the rightness of his country's cause, and a heart devoid of hate for fellow-men.

The thoughts to which he gave expression in the very few incomparable war sonnets which he has left behind will be shared by many thousands of young men moving resolutely and blithely forward into this, the hardest, the cruellest and the least rewarded of all the wars that men have fought. They are a whole history and revelation of Rupert Brooke himself. Joyous, fearless, versatile, deeply instructed, with classic symmetry of mind and body, he was all that one would wish England's noblest sons to be in days when no sacrifice but the most precious is acceptable, and the most precious is that which is most freely proffered.'

The trite, falsifying phrases of funeral rhetoric follow one another with appalling monotony. Churchill's orotund threnody gave the signal for an orgy of public lamentation in which his death, in spite of its pathetic and humiliating circumstances, was compared with the mortal wounds that Sidney received under the walls of Zutphen in 1586. Even Maynard Keynes, Gilbert Murray and D. H. Lawrence joined in the emotionalism of the shattering moment. Lawrence, in a letter to Lady Ottoline, wrote in his unique and extraordinary way:

> 'The death of Rupert Brooke fills me more and more with the sense of the fatuity of it all. He was slain by bright Phoebus' shaft – it was in keeping with his general sunniness – it was the real climax of his pose. I first heard of him as a Greek god under a Japanese sunshade, reading poetry in his pyjamas, at Grantchester – at Grantchester upon the lawns where the river goes. Bright Phoebus smote him down. It is all in the saga.
>
> O God, O God; it is all too much of a piece: it is like madness.'

A year later, Henry James, who had wept when he was told of Rupert's death, was invited to provide an introduction to the *Letters from America* which were published in 1916. Written when he was near his own death, and deeply stricken by the dangers which beset the civilization he loved so much, it is a sad piece of almost maudlin rhapsody which gave unchecked expression to the sentimental adulation of an older man for a romantic, good-looking younger man. More than most people, James was always liable to be overcome in the presence of youthful beauty, and was clearly smitten when he first met Rupert in Cambridge:

'He reappears to me as with his felicities all most promptly divinable, in that splendid setting of the river at the "Backs"; indeed I remember vaguely wondering what it was left for such a place to do with the added, the veritably wasted, grace of such a person.' He saw him as the 'ideal image of English youth', and claimed that he 'expressed us *all*, at the highest tide of our actuality'. It is to James's credit that, even in the full glow of his hero-worship, when Rupert was already on his way to the Dardanelles, his critical faculty was not altogether extinguished, and he could find fault with the sonnets in various detail when writing to Marsh about them. It was rather, it seems, as a reminder of the golden youth who was lost to him that he treasured them: 'This evening, alone by my lamp, I have been reading them over and over to myself aloud, as if fondly to test and truly to try them, almost in fact as if to reach the far-off author, in whatever unimaginable conditions, by some miraculous, some telepathic intimation that I am in quavering communication with him.' Now, in his introduction, he wrote, admittedly rather enigmatically: 'No young man had ever so naturally taken on under the pressure of life the poetic nature, and shaken it so free of every encumbrance by simply wearing it as he wore his complexion or his outline....Never was a young singer either less obviously sentimental or addicted to the mere twang of the guitar.'

That Rupert had died of sunstroke and blood poisoning before he ever reached the fighting was clearly an idea that was intolerable to James. He brushed it aside, and wrote: 'Rupert Brooke, young, happy, radiant, extraordinarily endowed and irresistibly attaching, virtually met a soldier's death, met it in the stress of action and the all but immediate presence of the enemy.' And he concluded on his highest note: 'It is perhaps even a touch beyond any dreamt-of harmony that, under omission of no martial honour, he was to be carried by comrades and devoted waiting sharers, whose evidence survives them, to the steep summit of a Greek island of infinite grace....'

In spite of this full orchestra of public legend-making, there were friends who quietly kept their heads. They saw a danger – and rightly as events were already proving – that a completely mythical character was going to be substituted for the highly complex and all too human person they had known. In the *Cambridge Magazine* E. J. Dent published a long article in which he wrote:

'It is grotesquely tragic – what a characteristic satire he would have written on it himself – that he should have died (at Lemnos too!*) just after a sudden and rather factitious celebrity had been obtained by a few poems which, beautiful as they are in technique and expression, represented him in a phase that could only have been temporary. No Englishman can ever quite eradicate the national tendency to romanticism, just as there is, according to Romain Rolland, an essential Massenet that slumbers in the heart of every true Frenchman. In the first shock of the moment that romanticism he so hated came uppermost.'

* The Admiralty signals came from Lemnos, and it was therefore at first thought that Rupert had died there.

In the same magazine, a fortnight later, Harold Monro showed
his disgust at the way Brooke was being used as a recruiting
poster – 'He did his duty. Will you do yours?' – and made the
uncomfortably accurate point that while very few people understand or care about poetry, a poet's *death* is something easy to
grasp and easy to sentimentalize over. 'His whole poetry,' wrote
Monro caustically, 'is full of the repudiation of sentimentalism'
– which was only partly true and certainly not of the last
sonnets – 'His death was not more lovely than his life.' Even
the romantic-hearted John Sheppard, Rupert's former tutor at
King's, wrote in the *Cambridge Review* : 'Though it is not easy,
we owe it to him not to comfort ourselves by letting our
thoughts dwell on a mythical being who was not Rupert, and
whose loss is therefore the easier to bear.'

The publication of *1914 and Other Poems*, which included
the Tahiti poems and the characteristic ironic levity of the
fish poem *Heaven*, should, one feels, have made the fashioners
of the heroic monument pause; but it was too late, and it is
very doubtful if 'the Deans and great-aunts who picture Brooke
as a kind of blend of General Gordon and Lord Tennyson,' as
the *New Statesman* aptly described them, took in the undertone
of anti-Christian mockery in *Heaven*. Some of his friends were
writing to one another in the same strain. In a letter to Stanley
Spencer, Gwen Raverat complained that the many articles
about Rupert which she had read 'might have been written
about King David, or Lord Byron, or Sophocles, or any other
young man that wrote verse and was good-looking.' She put
her finger on the crux of it all when she concluded that 'they
never got the faintest feeling of his being a human being at all.'

Public memorials were, of course, immediately proposed,
including a bust in Poets' Corner in Westminster Abbey (as it
took Byron nearly a century and a half to get into the Abbey,
perhaps this will still be erected). The dottiest suggestion, made
in all seriousness, was surely that the hands of the clock at
Grantchester should be fixed for ever at ten to three. Finally,
early in 1916, a plaque in Rugby Chapel was settled on, a
committee was formed, public subscriptions were invited by
an announcement in *The Times*, Schell's profile photograph
('your favourite actress,' as his friends called it) was indicated
as a model for the medallion to be sculpted by Havard Thomas,
and Eric Gill, whom Rupert had deeply admired, was engaged

to cut the lettering for the sonnet 'If I should die' below it. Next year the plaque was finished, and sent to Mrs Brooke. A grand public unveiling was proposed, but as by that time the Government was discouraging any unnecessary railway travel, it did not take place. The plaque was quietly set up in its place in the Chapel, and it was not until after the Armistice, in March 1919, that the unveiling was at last celebrated. A large number of Rupert's surviving friends, from Cambridge and from the world of the Poetry Bookshop, were present, though Dudley Ward and Ka Cox were both in Paris. The ceremony took place after a luncheon given by Mrs Brooke at Bilton Road, and Rupert's Commander-in-Chief on the Dardanelles expedition, Sir Ian Hamilton (who had subsequently been made a scapegoat for its total failure, and sacked), gave an address which struck the now inevitable exalted note: 'I have seen famous men and brilliant figures in my day, but never one so thrilling, so vital as that of our hero. Like a prince he would enter a room, like a prince quite unconscious of his own royalty, and by that mere act put a spell upon everyone around him.' This was followed by a giant tea-party for several hundreds in the New Big School, and a concert in the evening, in which choral settings of the sonnets, by Sidney Nicholson, were sung.

The year before, in July, Rupert's *Collected Poems* were at last published, with a Memoir by Marsh which became famous, and did as much as anything else to fix the image of the Soldier-Poet-Hero in the public mind. One writer (in the *Cambridge Review*) went so far as to say: 'A legend has been endorsed. This life slips by like a panorama of earth's loveliest experience.' Marsh must not be too much blamed for its excesses of adulation; he had known Rupert at close quarters in the last years of his life, he had fallen in love with him, and his love irradiates every paragraph. It was nevertheless of no genuine service to his dead friend. Everyone who bought the poems in this collected edition – and tens of thousands did so – naturally read the Memoir, and assumed it to be the definitive account of Rupert's life. What they could not know was not merely that the general picture was superficial and sentimental hagiography rather than dispassionate portraiture, but also that Marsh had little or no knowledge of the turbulence of Rupert's emotional life, especially in the period before he met Cathleen Nesbitt.

The Memoir passed through many re-writings before the final

version, chiefly because Marsh was at loggerheads with Mrs Brooke, who had felt for a long time that Marsh's influence had been bad for Rupert, taking him away from the wholesome ambience of his home, and above all introducing him to his 'London seasons'; and felt now, after his death, that Marsh was presuming too much on Rupert's last and unfortunately ambiguous letters about his literary executors and his papers in handling them all himself and making decisions that he had no real authority to make. She felt – and it is not difficult to understand her feeling – that Marsh was behaving almost as if he owned Rupert. After a long and often (on her part) acrimonious correspondence, she finally agreed to Marsh's fourth version in 1918, but with no good grace. She maintained at the last that she had not realized that the Memoir was to be as it were a preface to the collected poems, and on the grounds that most people would already have *Poems 1911* and *1914 and Other Poems* went so far as to call it a 'swindle'. She had her revenge by cutting Marsh out as an executor and appointing instead Geoffrey Keynes, John Sheppard, Dudley Ward, and, as a representative of the beneficiaries, Walter de la Mare. This came into force on her death in October 1930. One must also note that she ignored Rupert's own stipulation, or request, that after her death his papers should go to Ka Cox.

The paragon who emerges from the transforming pages of the Memoir, is a sunny, forever-laughing youth of flawless beauty and many-sided genius, the adored of all with whom he came into contact, of pure heart and stainless character. Marsh described the impression Rupert made on him when he first saw him on stage in the Greek Play Committee's production of the *Eumenides* during his first term, in an image which has haunted the minds of many and stuck in the gullets of others. Rupert had written to his mother, 'The idea of my playing Hermes fell through, but they have given me the equally large part of the Herald. I stand in the middle of the stage and pretend to blow a trumpet, while somebody in the wings makes a sudden noise. The part is not difficult.' In another letter he wrote, 'I wear a red wig and cardboard armour, and luckily am only visible for a minute.' It turned out that he was one of the successes of the evening. 'His radiant, youthful figure,' Marsh wrote, 'in gold and vivid red and blue, like a page in the Riccardi Chapel, stood strangely out against the stuffy decorations and dresses which pervaded those somewhat palmy days of the Cambridge Theatre. After eleven years, the impression is still vivid.'

In the Memoir Marsh allowed Rupert to speak for himself as far as possible by quotations from his letters, especially while he was on his American trip. To these he added quotations from what some of his contemporaries had written after his death, selecting the passages which reflected Rupert in the same glowing colours as he had used himself. Memorials written soon after the loss of a beloved friend can scarcely be other than nostalgic eulogies; but Rupert's close and always devoted friend Denis Browne, whose description of his death I have quoted in full, outdid all others when he wrote to Mrs Brooke while still shattered by his death, and only days before he was killed himself:

'No words of mine can tell you the sorrow of those he has left behind him here. No one of us knew him without loving him, whether they knew him for ten years, as I did, or for a couple of months as others. His brother officers and his men mourn him very deeply. But those who knew him chiefly as a poet of the rarest gifts, the brightest genius, know that the loss is not only yours and ours, but the world's. And beyond his genius there was that infinitely lovable soul, that stainless heart whose early death can only be the beginning of a true immortality.

To his friends Rupert stood for something so much purer, greater, and nobler than ordinary men that his loss seems more explicable than theirs. He has gone to where he came from; but if anyone left the world richer by passing through it, it was he.'

It was on this trumpet note that Marsh concluded his Memoir.

There was, however, one contemporary review of the book which made a brave attempt to redress the balance. It appeared in the *Times Literary Supplement* and was therefore anonymous, but many people soon came to guess that it was written by Virginia Woolf. She had long been a close friend of Ka Cox, who had marvellously aided Leonard when Virginia had her serious breakdown in 1913-14. She called her 'my Bruin', and had written to her in January 1916: 'I thought perhaps I was arrogant and scratchy in the way I talked of Rupert the other day. I never think his poetry good enough for him, but I did admire him very much indeed, and he always seemed to me a fully grown person among mummies and starvelings (which refers to the people I lived among). But it seems to me sometimes that our casual way of talking must sound silly to anyone like you who knew him really and therefore understood what he might do.'

When the article on Marsh's Memoir appeared in the *Times Literary Supplement* (8 August 1918), Ka evidently wrote to her to ask if she knew who the author was, probably suspecting the truth. Virginia replied: '*I* wrote the article on Rupert in the *Times*. Bruce Richmond sent the book to me; but when I came to do it I felt that to say out loud what even I knew of Rupert was utterly repulsive, so I merely trod my 2 columns as decorously as possible. It seemed useless to pitch into Eddie [Marsh]. James [Strachey] meant to try, but gave it up. I think it was one of the most repulsive biographies I've ever read (this is, of course, a little overstated!). He contrived to make the letters as superficial and affected as his own account of Rupert. We're now suggesting that James should write something for us to print. He's sending us the letters to look at.'

The review itself was indeed 'decorous', but Virginia's dislike of the book, and particularly of Marsh's sentimentality, does, it seems to me, come through pretty clearly. She begins by referring to his mother's attempt to get some of his contemporaries to collaborate, and its failure, and Marsh's consequent regret that the memoir was 'of necessity incomplete'. She goes on :

'It is inevitably incomplete, as Mr. Marsh, we are sure, would be the first to agree, if for no other reason because it is the work of an older man. A single sentence brings this clearly before us. No undergraduate of Rupert Brooke's own age would have seen "his radiant youthful figure in gold and vivid red and blue, like a page in the Riccardi Chapel"; that is the impression of an older man. The contemporary version would have been less pictorial and lacking in the half-humorous tenderness which is so natural an element in the mature vision of beautiful and gifted youth. There would have been less of the vivid red and blue and gold, more that was mixed, particoloured and matter for serious debate. In addition Mr. Marsh has had to face the enormous difficulties

which beset the biographers of those who have died with
undeveloped powers, tragically, and in the glory of public
gratitude. They leave so little behind them that can serve to
recall them with an exactitude. A few letters, written from
school and college, a fragment of a diary – that is all. The
power of expressing oneself naturally in letters comes to
most people late in life. Rupert Brooke wrote freely, but not
altogether without self-consciousness, and it is evident that
his friends have not cared to publish the more intimate passages in his letters to them. Inevitably, too, they have not
been willing to tell the public the informal things by which
they remember him best. With these serious and necessary
drawbacks Mr. Marsh has done his best to present a general
survey of Rupert Brooke's life which those who knew him
will be able to fill in here and there more fully, perhaps a
little to the detriment of the composition as a whole. But
they will be left, we believe, to reflect rather sadly upon the
incomplete version which must in future represent Rupert
Brooke to those who never knew him.'

Rupert's mother evidently found out that Virginia had written
the review, and wrote to her about it. Virginia wrote back
rather cautiously, fearing to upset Mrs Brooke:

'I had rather hoped that you would *not* see my review, as
I felt that I had not been able to say what I wanted to say
about Rupert. Also I am afraid that I gave the impression that
I disliked Mr. Marsh's memoir much more than I meant to.
If I was at all disappointed it was that he gave of course
rather his impression of Rupert than the impression which
one had always had of him partly from the Stracheys and
other friends of his own age. But then Mr. Marsh could not
have done otherwise, and one is very glad to have the
Memoir as it is. Rupert was so great a figure in his friends
eyes that no memoir could possibly be good enough. Indeed
I felt it to be useless to try to write about him. One couldn't
get near to his extraordinary charm and goodness. I was 5
years older than he was, and I saw him very little in comparison with most people, but perhaps because of the St
Ives days I always felt that I knew him as one knows one's
own family. I stayed a week at Grantchester [1911] and then

he came down here [Asheham House in Sussex], and we met sometimes in London. He was a wonderful friend.'

The entry in her Diary had been in a very different tone, echoed in her letter to Ka a few weeks later. She was reporting a conversation with Lytton Strachey and Dora Carrington at their house at Tidmarsh: 'A great deal of talk about Rupert. The book is a disgraceful sloppy sentimental rhapsody, leaving Rupert rather tarnished.'

In her review, confined inevitably by the space such an article could be allowed, she endeavoured to give her own assessment of Rupert's character and qualities. It is done with Virginia's usual sharp perception and imaginative understanding, and I think it may stand as the fairest summing-up by an intelligent contemporary who had also been a friend for many long years.

After the opening sentences I have already quoted, she goes on first to recall her personal connection with Rupert, though not mentioning the childhood encounters at St Ives:

'The remembrance of a week spent in his company, of a few meetings in London and the country, offers a tantalizing fund of memories at once very definite, very little related to the Rupert Brooke of legend, presenting each one an extremely clear sense of his presence, but depending so much upon that presence and upon other circumstances inextricably involved with it, that one may well despair of rendering a clear account to a third person, let alone to a multiple of many such people as the general public.

But the outline at least is clear enough. So much has been written of his personal beauty that to state one's first impression of him in that respect needs some audacity, since the first impression was of a type so conventionally handsome and English as to make it inexpressive or expressive only of something that one might be inclined half-humorously to disparage. He was the type of English young manhood at its healthiest and most vigorous. Perhaps at the particular stage he had then reached, following upon the decadent phase of his first Cambridge Days, he emphasized this purposely; he was consciously and defiantly pagan. He was living at Grantchester; his feet were permanently bare; he disdained tobacco and butcher's meat; and he lived all day, and perhaps slept all night, in the open air. You might judge him extreme, and from the pinnacle of superior age assure him that the return to Nature was as sophisticated as any other pose, but you could not from the first moment of speech with him doubt that, whatever he might do, he was an originator, one of those leaders who spring up from time to time and show their power most clearly by subjugating their own genera-tion. Under his influence the country near Cambridge was full of young men and women walking barefoot, sharing his passion for bathing and fish diet, disdaining book learning, and proclaiming that there was something deep and wonder-ful in the man who brought the milk and in the woman who watched the cows. . . . But however sunburnt and slap-dash he might choose to appear at any particular moment, no one could know him even slightly without seeing that he was not only very sincere, but passionately in earnest about the things he cared for. In particular, he cared for literature and the art of writing as seriously as it is possible to care for them. He had read everything and he had read it from the point of view of a working writer. . . . You felt that to him literature was not dead nor of the past, but a thing now in process of construction by people many of whom were his friends; and that knowledge, skill, and, above all, unceasing hard work were required of those who attempt to make it. To work hard, much harder than most writers think it necessary, was an injunction of his that remains in memory from a chaos of such discussions.'

In a review that strikes one as surprisingly intimate and personal for the generally reticent and impersonal pages of the *Times Literary Supplement*, she goes on to describe some-thing even more closely personal, a scene which took place while she was staying at Grantchester; though she does not say – what we know from other sources – that the image of 'a leaf in the sun' was in fact proposed spontaneously by herself:

'The proofs of his first book of poems were lying about that summer on the grass. There were also the manuscripts of poems that were in process of composition. It seemed natural to turn his poetry over and say nothing about it, save per-haps to remark upon his habit of leaving spaces for unforth-coming words which gave his manuscript the look of a puzzle

with a number of pieces missing. On one occasion he wished
to know what was the brightest thing in nature? And then,
deciding with a glance round him that the brightest thing
was a leaf in the sun, a blank space towards the end of "Town
and Country" was filled in immediately
  Cloud-like we lean and stare as bright leaves stare.
  But instead of framing any opinion as to the merit of
his verses we recall merely the curiosity of watching him
finding his adjective, and a vague conception that he was
somehow a mixture of scholar and man of action, and
that his poetry was the brilliant by-product of energies not
yet turned upon their object. It may seem strange, now that
he is famous as a poet, how little it seemed to matter in
those days whether he wrote poetry or not. It is proof perhaps
of the exciting variety of his gifts and of the immediate
impression he made of being so complete and remarkable
in himself that it was sufficient to think of him merely as
Rupert Brooke. . . . His practical ability, which was often a
support to his friends, was one of the gifts that seemed to
mark him for success in active life. He was keenly aware of
the state of public affairs, and if you chanced to meet him
when there was talk of a strike or an industrial dispute he
was evidently as well versed in the complications as in the
obscurities in the poetry of Donne. . . . It needed no special
intimacy to guess that beneath "an appearance almost of
placidity" he was the most restless, complex, and analytic of
human beings. It was impossible to think of him withdrawn,
abstracted or indifferent. Whether or not it was for the good
of his poetry he would be in the thick of things, and one
fancies that he would in the end have framed a speech that
came very close to the modern point of view – a subtle
analytic poetry, or prose perhaps, full of intellect, and full of
his keen unsentimental curiosity.'

Virginia Woolf concludes her remarkable article, so penetrating, so sympathetic and sceptical at the same time, with
the remark that cannot have pleased the worshippers of the
figment of their imagination, the fulfilled poet and patriot hero :
'one turns from him not with a sense of completeness and
finality, but rather to wonder and question still : what would
he have been, what would he have done ?'

Virginia Woolf was, of course, painting a portrait of the Rupert she had known before his breakdown, though she must have heard of what had happened from the Stracheys or Ka Cox herself. It is good to think that his last encounter with her was one that implied at least a measure of reconciliation, as if he had suddenly been overcome by the feeling that his attitude had been absurd and unjust, even more unjust than in the cases of his other former friends who were also friends of hers – to include her in his unreasoning vendetta against Bloomsbury. In the third volume of his autobiography, *Beginning Again*, Leonard Woolf describes the occasion: 'In 1915, just before he went out to the Dardanelles and died in the Aegean, walking down Holborn one morning we met him by chance. We stopped to talk and for the first moment there was hostility and even anger in his look and voice. But almost immediately they seemed to evaporate, and he was suddenly friendly and charming and we went into a nearby restaurant and had lunch. He was gay and affectionate, just as he had been that first evening in Cambridge.'

It was one of Rupert's many misfortunes at this time to die before the appalling carnage on the Western Front utterly changed the mood in which the young soldiers could write of the war. Siegfried Sassoon, Wilfred Owen and Isaac Rosenberg are rightly thought of as the outstanding poets of this second phase of the fighting; and the atmosphere of their poems, bitter, disillusioned, starkly realistic, inspired by the futility of the unbelievable suffering to which the troops were being exposed, and by the consequent desire to make the civilians in Britain aware at last of this reality, is immeasurably far away from the mellifluous versifying and romantic attitudinizing of the 1914 sonnets. It seems scarcely possible that this highly sensitive writer, who had shown himself in earlier poems so impatient of decorous pretences, would not have felt challenged, in spite of his new friendships with the politicians and soldiers in high places who were directing the war, to tell the truth about the Gallipoli fighting as Sassoon and Owen were to tell it about the Western Front. That is, if he had survived it; for most of the friends with whom he had journeyed out on that doomed expedition were either killed on the beaches, or elsewhere soon after. By the end of June the Hood battalion had lost eleven of its fifteen officers, including Denis Browne. Of the original group of soldier friends the only two to survive the war were 'Oc', as Brigadier General Arthur Asquith DSO, and Freyberg, as a Major-General with a VC as well as a DSO. As Virginia Woolf wrote, one is left for ever with the question : what would he have been, what would he have done?

Postscript

The elements which create a legend around a particular person, whether man of affairs, soldier, artist or poet, are diverse and often mysterious. They do not seem to be entirely rational or predictable. Frequently the legend survives subsequent historical debunking, or the revelation of facts about the legendary person which are far from favourable to his (or her) character and cast doubts on his (or her) hitherto assumed achievements.

Rupert Brooke, like T. E. Lawrence, is one of those rare legendary figures in the English story during the present century. He became a legend from the moment the Dean of St Paul's, at a crucial period of discouragement and anxiety for Britain in the First World War, quoted one of his sonnets in his Easter sermon in 1915. Brooke's death in the Aegean very soon after, as he was about to take part in the ill-starred Gallipoli landings, and the glorifying obituary Winston Churchill wrote for him in *The Times*, reinforced the deep impression the Easter sermon had made. After the edition of *New Numbers* was rapidly exhausted the sonnets were published in *1914 and Other Poems*, and sold at once, and continued to sell, in tens and eventually hundreds of thousands. The English public, the fathers, mothers, wives, lovers and friends of the men who were involved in the fighting – in a way that the civilian population of all classes had never before been engaged in an acute war situation – found, as I have already suggested, in the sentiments expressed in the famous five sonnets, without analysing them too deeply, an expression rather of their ideal dream of what England stood for in the conflict and of what they hoped the men who were being killed at such an appalling rate in the bloody theatres of war were gaining by their sacrifice, rather than any intimation of stark reality.

In a sensitive and sympathetic (though not uncritical) broadcast written in 1952 before Hassall's biography came out, the poet Patric Dickinson said: 'They are not very good poems,' but 'Brooke's "place in poetry" does not matter half as much as this catalytic quality.' The name 'Rupert Brooke' became invested then with an aura, a magic that still survives, even amongst a multitude of people who may not even have read the sonnets, or know anything about the life of their author. Every intelligent young person in whom a taste for poetry has been awakened in his school or undergraduate days knows something of the poems, and has heard of the little Cambridgeshire village of Grantchester; though he may know something of the later poets of the First World War, who are now much more highly prized, or the very different poets of the Second World War. This does not mean that the legend is indestructible. It is nevertheless remarkable that during the Spanish Civil War there were some in Britain who liked to see in John Cornford (his first name was Rupert) the equivalent of Rupert Brooke as representing the idealism that Civil War inspired among liberals and socialists; while at the outbreak of the second war some elderly publicists lamented the lack of a Rupert Brooke to idealize the new catastrophe. Even now, more than sixty years after Brooke's death, that day of mourning for his friends is commemorated in the leading English newspapers, as the deaths of Florence Nightingale and Lord Byron and others of the chosen few in the English roll of honour are commemorated. On the more ludicrous side, one can record the fact that in the Old Orchard in Grantchester, a place that owes its fame entirely to Brooke, on a fine Sunday afternoon in summer more than 800 teas are sometimes served to the tourists from the sightseeing coaches.

Of course his great physical beauty, which struck everyone who met him, and the extraordinary magnetic charm, which was felt by almost everyone in his various circles of friends, supported and enhanced the effect of the sonnets. And yet when the legend was born in the spring of 1915 very few people knew what he looked like or had seen the Schell photographs, which were soon after used as a frontispiece to his posthumous volume of poems and later became an integral part of the popular dream; nor had any of the subsequent hero-worshipping memorials, such as Edward Marsh's or Sybil Pye's, been printed.

What the myth-creating public had to go on was little more than what Churchill had written: that Rupert Brooke was 'joyous, fearless, versatile, deeply instructed, with classic symmetry of mind and body'.

In fact, for the birth of the legend, it comes back to the sonnets. And the deep irony of it is that in the many books that have been written in recent years about the poetry of the First World War, in the introductions to the increasing number of anthologies, and among the studies of the English literary scene of the first quarter of this century, scarcely a word of more than heavily qualified praise, if that, can be found for them.

In his *English Poetry of the First World War* (1964) John H. Johnston writes: 'Elegant, melodious, rich in texture, decorous and dignified in tone, the 1914 sonnets do not deal with war; they reveal a sophisticated sensibility contemplating itself on the verge of war. Like Wordsworth's impassioned sonnets of 1802, Brooke's 1914 was inspired by a great moral and social crisis, but instead of defining that crisis, as Wordsworth does, in national and historical terms, Brooke merely presents its effects on his own rather specialized range of response.' After a rather destructive analysis of the individual sonnets, Johnston quotes with approval Charles Sorley's judgement on the whole sequence. Again, in his *Men Who March Away* (1965) Ian Parsons, who calls the first section of his anthology *Visions of Glory*, writes: 'This was the period of euphoria, when it was still possible to believe that war was a tolerably chivalrous affair, offering welcome opportunities for heroism and self-sacrifice, and to hope that this particular war would be over in six months. Rupert Brooke's 1914 sonnets are the apotheosis of this attitude, and though they seem to me to suffer from a crippling shallowness of feeling, and to be correspondingly facile in expression, it is undeniable that they said something to the men who went off to fight, and be killed in the early years of the war.' And Bernard Bergonzi, in his *Heroes' Twilight* (also 1965), writes:

'The sonnets themselves are not very amenable to critical discussion. They are works of very great mythic power, since they formed a unique focus for what the English felt, or wanted to feel, in 1914–15; they crystallize the powerful archetype of Brooke, the young Apollo, in his sacrificial role of the hero-as-victim. Considered, too, as historical documents, they are of interest as an index to the popular state of mind in the early months of the war. But considered more narrowly and exactly as poems, their inadequacy is very patent. . . . Brooke's poetic gifts were never very robust, and he was very far from being the most talented of the Georgian group, but at his best he had a certain irony and detachment of mind, which, very naturally, were absent from the 1914 sonnets. At the same time, the negative aspects of his poetry, a dangerous facility of language and feeling, are embarrassingly in evidence.'

The attitude of the latest anthologist and critic, Jon Silkin, in his rather wordy and over-theoretical introduction to the *Penguin Book of First World War Poetry* (1979), is distinctly more scathing. He sees Brooke as the representative *par excellence* of the first of four stages of consciousness about the war among its poets, and writes: 'Not so much a stage in consciousness as a passive reflection of, or conduit for, the prevailing patriotic ideas, and the cant that's contingent on most social abstract impulses. Brooke fairly offers a version of this.'

I am inclined to prefer Michael Hastings's 'If he is to be judged as a war poet alone, God help his image and his worth!' In his biography, *The Handsomest Young Man in England* (1967), he goes on, with perceptive fairness, to point out that the reaction against and in fact the almost total dismissal of the 1914 sonnets nowadays by critics and modern poets alike (with the exception of his chief biographer, Christopher Hassall, who is almost ecstatic about them) is in danger of sweeping away with them the good poems that Rupert Brooke *did* write, such as *Tiare Tahiti*, *Mummia*, the *Fish* poems and the brilliantly clever light verse of *Grantchester*, and justly observes that 'it is the *unfulfilment* in his pleasant, remarkable personality which is of importance and must continue to be.'

E. J. Dent, who knew him so well, and whose observations I have already quoted in this book, thought that the sonnets, 'beautiful as they are in technique and expression, represent him only in a phase that could only have been temporary'. To what extent that temporary phase would have been succeeded, if he had lived, by a new phase that would have done justice to his true abilities, Rupert Brooke seems to have been as uncertain as his friend Virginia Woolf. The last long *Fragment*, written in the Aegean shortly before he died, before the four lines I have already quoted in an earlier chapter, does indeed to my mind suggest a change in his mood and thinking, far away from the rhetoric of the sonnets:

I strayed about the deck, an hour, to-night
Under a cloudy moonless sky; and peeped
In at the windows, watched my friends at table,
Or playing cards, or standing in the doorway,
Or coming out into the darkness. Still
No one could see me.

I would have thought of them
– Heedless, within a week of battle – in pity,
Pride in their strength and in the weight and firmness
And link'd beauty of bodies, and pity that
This gay machine of splendour'ld soon be broken,
Thought little of, pashed, scattered. . . .

Only, always,
I could but see them – against the lamplight – pass
Like coloured shadows, thinner than filmy glass,
Slight bubbles, fainter than the wave's faint light,
That broke to phosphorous out in the night,
Perishing things and strange ghosts – soon to die
To other ghosts – this one, or that, or I.

Perhaps, if he had survived into 1917 and 1918, he would have dismissed the legend himself more ruthlessly than anyone else. Perhaps only he could have done it – and been disbelieved.

Main Books Consulted

By Rupert Brooke

Poems 1911
Georgian Poetry 1911–12
Georgian Poetry 1913–15
Collected Poems, with Memoir by E. Marsh (1918)
The Poetical Works, ed. Geoffrey Keynes (1946)
John Webster and the Elizabethan Drama (1916)
Letters from America, with Preface by Henry James (1916)
The Prose (selected), ed. Christopher Hassall (1956)
The Letters (selected), ed. Geoffrey Keynes (1968)

About Rupert Brooke

Rupert Brooke and the Intellectual Imagination
   by Walter de la Mare (1919)
A Number of People
   by Edward Marsh (1938)
The Golden Echo
   by David Garnett (1953)
The Flowers of the Forest
   by David Garnett (1956)
Edward Marsh: a Biography
   by Christopher Hassall (1959)
Rupert Brooke: a Biography
   by Christopher Hassall (1964)
Winston Churchill as I Knew Him
   by Lady Violet Bonham-Carter (1965)
The Handsomest Young Man in England
   by Michael Hastings (1967)

The Georgian Revolt
  by Robert Ross (1967)
Lytton Strachey: Vol. 1, the Unknown Years
  by Michael Holroyd (1967)
Rupert Brooke: a Reappraisal and Selection
  by Timothy Rogers (1971)
Virginia Woolf: a Biography, Vol. 1
  by Quentin Bell (1972)
A Little Love and Good Company
  by Cathleen Nesbitt (1974)
The Letters of Virginia Woolf, Vol. 2
  ed. Nigel Nicolson and Joanne Trautmann (1976)
The Diary of Virginia Woolf, Vol. 1
  ed. Anne Olivier Bell (1977)
Books and Portraits
  by Virginia Woolf, ed. Mary Lyon (1977)

Index

PR
6003
.R4
Z69
1980

A.L. OLIVEIRA MEMORIAL LIBRARY

3 1782 00045 5606

PR6003 .R4 Z69 1980
The strange destiny of Rupert B
rooke / c1980

12/80